The Second Best Bed

Recent Titles in
Contributions to the Study of World Literature

Darkness at Heart: Fathers and Sons in Conrad
Catharine Rising

Naguib Mahfouz's Egypt: Existential Themes in His Writings
Haim Gordon

Comic Tales of the Middle Ages: An Anthology and Commentary
Marc Wolterbeek

Framing the *Canterbury Tales:* Chaucer and the Medieval Frame Narrative Tradition
Katharine S. Gittes

There Is No Truer Truth: The Musical Aspect of Browning's Poetry
Nachum Schoffman

Reworlding: The Literature of the Indian Diaspora
Emmanuel S. Nelson, editor

Caliban in Exile: The Outsider in Caribbean Fiction
Margaret Paul Joseph

Sitting at the Feet of the Past: Retelling the North American Folktale for Children
Gary D. Schmidt and Donald R. Hettinga, editors

The Anna Book: Searching for Anna in Literary History
Mickey Pearlman, editor

Writing and Reality: A Study of Modern British Diary Fiction
Andrew Hassam

Shakespeare's Proverbial Themes: A Rhetorical Context for the Sententia as *Res*
Marjorie Donker

Promptings of Desire: Creativity and the Religious Impulse in the Works of D. H. Lawrence
Paul Poplawski

THE SECOND BEST BED

Shakespeare's Will in a New Light

JOYCE ROGERS

Contributions to the Study of World Literature, Number 48

Greenwood Press
Westport, Connecticut • London

Library of Congress Cataloging-in-Publication Data

Rogers, Joyce.
The second best bed : Shakespeare's will in a new light / Joyce Rogers.
p. cm.—(Contributions to the study of world literature, ISSN 0738-9345 ; no. 48)
Includes bibliographical references and index.
ISBN 0-313-28831-3 (alk. paper)
1. Shakespeare, William, 1564–1616—Will. 2. Probate law and practice—England—Stratford-upon-Avon—History—17th century.
3. Wills—England—Stratford-upon-Avon—History—17th century.
4. Dramatists, English—Early modern, 1500–1700—Biography.
5. Stratford-upon-Avon (England)—Social life and customs.
I. Title. II. Series.
PR2908.R64 1993
822.3′3—dc20 92-33763

British Library Cataloguing in Publication Data is available.

Library of Congress Catalog Card Number: 92–33763
ISBN: 0-313-28831-3
ISSN: 0738-9345

First published in 1993

Greenwood Press, 88 Post Road West, Westport, CT 06881
An imprint of Greenwood Publishing Group, Inc.

Printed in the United States of America

The paper used in this book complies with the Permanent Paper Standard issued by the National Information Standards Organization (Z39.48-1984).

10 9 8 7 6 5 4 3 2 1

To my family, friends, and *alma mater,*
Texas Christian University

et in memoriam
Professor Lorraine Sherley

Enter Time, *the* Chorus.

Time. I, that please some, try all, both joy and terror
Of good and bad, that makes and unfolds error,
Now take upon me, in the name of Time,
To use my wings. . . . it is in my pow'r
To o'erthrow law, and in one self-born hour
To plant and o'erwhelm custom. Let me pass
The same I am, ere ancient'st order was
Or what is now receiv'd. I witness to
The times that brought them in; so shall I do
To th'freshest things now reigning, and make stale
The glistering of this present, as my tale
Now seems to it.

—*The Winter's Tale,* IV.i.1–15

Contents

Illustrations

Preface

"The law hath not been dead, though it hath slept."
Measure for Measure, II.ii.90

Seldom in literary history has any document received the attention given Shakespeare's last will and testament. Since its devisement over three centuries ago, scores of articles and books have been written in an attempt to interpret what scholars have noted as its obscurities. Indeed, about this area of Shakespearean scholarship, it would appear, nothing more can be said.

Yet there is more to be said. New light can be brought to bear upon the dramatist's last public words by a study of medieval and Renaissance legal backgrounds which bear upon the will.

True, this area, too, like the subject of the will itself, has been worked over and over, though largely by legal historians concerned either with Shakespeare's knowledge of and/or involvement in the law or with the legality of the will in general. Scholars are all familiar with the studies representative of this line of research, beginning with the early ones like those of Edmond Malone in his 1790 edition *Shakespere, Plays and Poems* and F. J. Furnivall in his Introduction to *The Royal Shakespere* (1880). Following these, the case for Shakespeare's involvement in the law has gained credibility on the basis of evidence brought forward from plays and records of litigation, leading in some instances to full-blown assertions that Shakespeare was in fact a lawyer, such as those by William Rushton in *Shakespeare: A Lawyer* (1858), John Campbell in *Shakespeare's Legal Acquirements Considered* (1859), and more recently O. Hood Phillips in *Shakespeare and the Lawyers* (1972).[1] As to Shakespeare's knowledge of the law, facsimiles of Records of the Stratford Court of Record alluding to cases that would certainly have been within Shakespeare's purveyance—involving as they did either himself or his family—are included in S. Schoenbaum's *William Shakespeare: Records and Images* (1981; 59ff.).

Indeed it would be difficult to find a Shakespearean scholar who has not dealt with the legal or other problems having to do with Shakespeare's will.

Yet, though the findings of my study strongly support the belief that Shakespeare was either very well-advised or very well up on the law, the degree of his involvement with the law is not the issue here. Moreover, while the legal documents of the time which serve as primary sources for my study do give legal answer to the doubts and speculations that have grown up around the will in the centuries since its devisement and do go far toward resolving its obscurities, the legal incontestability was neither the primary concern of the will nor is it mine.

What has not been done and what I am going to do is to subject the problems of the will to a comparative point-by-point analysis with the standard testamentary sourcebook of the day and examine old ecclesiastical laws as a source for background. I will show how the will is replete with elements of civil and common as well as ecclesiastical law and custom. The results of such a study will make more understandable the disputed points of Shakespeare's will and at the same time establish that the will was as correct, incontestable, and conventional as possible and that even the phrase "second best" was in accordance with the law and custom of his time.

The focus of my study, however, is not on the law as such but rather on how the law was brought into the service of Shakespeare's family for whom the will was written. Shakespeare used the law of the will to serve the best interests and meet the needs of the women and the children in his family as well as the friends named therein, to acknowledge their relationship to the testator, and to serve their needs by the securement of the provisions made therein. Shakespeare's legal preoccupations at the time the will was devised were subordinate to his concern for the women in his family and for his future heirs. There are, for example, personal touches, however small, which interpreters have not noticed but which would not have been lost on those for whom the will was written.

After all, it was not intended as a controversial, cryptically devised document. There is nothing to indicate that it was obscure to those directly affected by it at the time of its devisement, even if to others of subsequent times and places it has proved to be an enigma. Its obscurity may be traced in large part to the fact that the laws and customs governing its formulation were in the process of becoming obsolete at the very time it was being drafted, and that their meanings were soon thereafter all but buried from view. As Shakespeare expressed it in the line from *Measure for Measure* that I selected as text for my introduction, the law "hath slept."

As I see it, the will presents an interpretive problem, which, as E. D. Hirsch, Jr., notes in *Validity in Interpretation,* "requires its own distinct context of relevant knowledge."[2]

In the case of the interpretation of Shakespeare's will the relevant knowledge encompasses both legal and literary history.

The law at the time Shakespeare was writing was in a state of transition. Some things were going out and some things were still observed, though diminished in force. The changes affected testamentary law as well as testamentary proceedings. In order to highlight the significance of the changes, I provide extensive background material on English legal history. At times I dwell on specific, often minute details such as legal interpretations of laws that are to be found in the marginalia of a text or studies in the evolution of meanings for legal words and/or phrases, the latter minutiae being of particular importance with regard to the phrase "second best."

It should be understood however that my stance is not from the vantage point of a lawyer but rather from that of a literary person. A legal reader with a legal background might find my overview cursory, for I may have left out some area of law or other. On the other hand, there is a danger that my literary colleagues will regard the legal data as far too prolix and irrelevant to modern concern (I will sound like last century's Bard scholar).

The literary scholar might also find the biographical information I bring out to be all too familiar. Yet, to vivify the reader's sense of the presence and personality of the women, children, and men who had been at the center of Shakespeare's life as he faced death, some reiteration might be necessary and I trust will be excused.

Chapter One focuses on the will, its contents, and the major controversies that have arisen over it. The original is on public display, though a number of facsimiles have been made, the best in my opinion being that reproduced in S. Schoenbaum's *William Shakespeare: A Documentary Life* (243–45). However, deciphering the English hand of the original is extremely difficult, even for those experienced in the paleography of the period. Therefore, I have thought it best to provide my own transcription of the will (Figure 1 in Chapter One). The transcription presented here retains original spelling, capitalization, absence of punctuation, and, to my knowledge, something unique to transcriptions of the will, lines and pages in accordance with those of the original. To preserve lines and pages, however, it has been necessary to reduce the text.

After reviewing the will's contents with the reader, I summarize the major points that have brought about scholarly controversy. These deal with peculiarities of the material condition of the manuscript, the irregularity of testamentary form signalled by such things as the unusual number of witnesses, and the seemingly quixotic choice of bequest and beneficiary. In order to take the reader beyond the stage of merely knowing the facts of the case, so to speak, I situate the will in its context of time and place, noting events relevant to the time during which it was drafted. Here I introduce the reader to a few of the major events touching Shakespeare's family life in the years leading up to his final illness and the devisement of the will. (In a later chapter I recreate more of the poet's family history for the entire ten-year period preceding his death in order to provide a backdrop for final resolution of the controversies.)

In Chapter Two I relate the controversial obscurities in the will and questions about family relationships to a point-by-point analysis of certain civil laws. I show how the will conforms to Elizabethan testamentary law. I further argue that the force of precedent from Roman civil law of antiquity is operative in the retention of requisites essential to the Solemn Testament, a legal form which explains several of the so-called problems. These are: the emended form of the will; the unusual number of witnesses; the apparent inequities of inheritance between the daughters; and the exclusion of his wife as primary beneficiary. In fact, as I demonstrate, the documents of the time show what has been viewed as doting paternal peculiarity and favoritism in the will's bequests to have been a shrewd use of common legal tactics to ensure familial protection.

In Chapter Three I set the will in the context of the times in which it was devised, showing the legal changes that were transpiring at the time. I make the further claim that the presence of overlapping legal elements in the will is typical of the developing state of affairs in the legal system of Shakespeare's day. It was a highly significant point in legal history when the very ground of English law was shifting. Civil and ecclesiastical law were being supplanted by modern common law. By learning even in a general way something about the background of English law and the shifts taking place within the legal system of Shakespeare's day, the reader will gain an appreciation of the legal astuteness of his will and understand why my study so heavily concentrates upon the importance of the old laws to the interpretation of the will. I show that the old laws and sourcebooks I use as the basis for my interpretation were very much before the public eye in many areas of life in Renaissance England.

I present strong evidence for establishing that Shakespeare and his family had personal ties with these and other areas of life in which the old laws were kept alive. This evidence further substantiates the claims made in my study that the will is best read in the context of medieval and Renaissance legal backgrounds.

In Chapter Four I deal specifically with the notorious bequest, showing the way in which the will also reflects the religious nature of wills in their ecclesiastical origins. In the bequest of the "second best bed," something very old is echoed in formulaic mode, namely, the ancient law of retributory tithe which, by Shakespeare's day, had become a testamentary custom. Thus, the infamous phrase "second best," so often taken as an intentionally malicious slur, may be understood in ancient context as a parting tribute of profound meaning.

Finally, in Chapter Five, I close the study by returning to the will as a family testament. By presenting the known biographical details of the poet's last years in sheer chronological succession, I hope to bring into focus the increasing family orientation of the poet's final years leading up to the drafting of the will. Thus seen or set within the personal scheme of things, the will, its legacies, the interlineations, remembrances, people named therein—all take us beyond artist, beyond legal astuteness, beyond controversy, to a man facing death, securing provision and legacy for family and friends. When the reader sees how intensely Shakespeare was involved in one family concern after another in the final years of his life, I believe any doubts still remaining as to the validity of the claims presented in my interpretation of the will as family testament may be settled.

In presenting evidence I often quote at what to some readers may seem an inordinate length. Quotation is extensive, particularly in the sections drawing upon major historical sources like Swinburne's treatise on testamentary law and Lambarde's collection of Anglo-Saxon laws. I have deliberately adopted this method, mainly to establish the longevity of the laws under discussion, but also to make immediately accessible to the reader material that is not widely known, not having been brought forward in this context before, or material that exists in unique manuscript form housed in special collections such as the Folger Shakespeare Library in Washington, D.C., and the Bodleian of Oxford University. In any case, much of the material is likely to be the last kind of thing one would ever have need to seek out in an ordinary lifetime and so I amply proffer it here.

Similarly, it may appear that I am overly concerned with pursuing words and phrases back to Anglo-Saxon times and earlier, but in the interpretation of legal language the meanings for words must be known, especially if the word in question is an archaic one. And the pursuit may be even more strongly justified when the very extent of time over which a given usage can be traced is a basis of proof for the validity of the proposed interpretation.

Acknowledgments

''One sows, another reaps''—these words certainly apply to my work on this book. Since its beginnings in 1981, from Anglo-Saxonists, medievalists, Shakespeare scholars, legal historians, and antiquarians in all fields, I have reaped a harvest, one which others worked for, and I have simply ''come into the rewards of their trouble'' (John 4:37–38).

By far the most pleasant part of completing a project of this size is acknowledging the many individuals who helped to make it possible. I would like to express first my appreciation to a number of people who have assisted me in this undertaking in very particular ways: to Marta Field for converting the manuscript from drafts into polished computer formatted pages; to Barbara Mowat, Director, Laetitia Yeandle, and Lena Orlin at the Folger Shakespeare Library in Washington, D.C., for assisting my work with the Lambarde *Archaionomia*; to John Barton, Reader in Roman Law at Merton College, Oxford University, for aiding my search into the testamentary *sed cum paulatim* at the Bodleian Law Library; to Dr. John Post, Assistant Deputy Keeper of the Records, Public Record Office, Chancery Lane, London, England, for giving me the opportunity to work directly with Shakespeare's will during my visit, especially since the will was not on display owing to remodelling of the building; to Dorothy Bethurum Loomis, for commenting helpfully on the Anglo Saxon sections and to Vincent Maddalen for enhancing my translations into English from Latin; and to Beatrice Hight and Dorothy Wonsmos, for acquiring reference and interlibrary loan sources needed for my research. Cathryn Lee and Diane Spalding, who read this manuscript for Greenwood Press, have provided careful and patient editorial assistance.

I am grateful to colleagues who read parts of the manuscript at various stages of revision and offered valuable suggestions: the late George Arms, Edith

Buchanan, David McPherson, and Janice Schuetz; and to many friends and colleagues whose advice and support helped me on countless occasions, especially Andrew Burgress. Marvin and Helga Spevack have offered ongoing encouragement of the project, as have Kathleen Matthews, Clare Intress, Jerome Shea, Mary Bess Whidden, Angela Boone, and Walther and Clare Volbach. I owe a special debt to Helen Damico, for giving of her time and knowledge in a careful reading from which this book greatly benefits.

Finally, I am most grateful to my mother, who generously provided financial and every other kind of support for my study and travel.

Abbreviations

Works frequently cited will be identified by the following abbreviations (see the list of Works Cited for complete facts of publication).

AS Charters	A. J. Robertson, *Anglo-Saxon Charters.*
AS Wills	*Anglo-Saxon Wills,* ed. Dorothy Whitelock.
BRL	Benjamin Roland Lewis, *The Shakespeare Documents,* 2 vols.
Brief Lives	John Aubry, *Aubrey's Brief Lives.*
Coke on Littleton	Sir Edward Coke, *The First Part of the Institutes of the Lawes of England; or, A Commentarie upon Littleton, not the name of a Lawyer onely, but of the Law it selfe.*
Commentaries	Sir William Blackstone, *Commentaries on the Laws of England* (facsimile 1765–69); Vol. II: *Of The Rights Of Things.*
Comp Doc Life	S. Schoenbaum, *William Shakespeare: A Compact Documentary Life.*
Doc Life	S. Schoenbaum, *William Shakespeare: A Documentary Life.*
Eccles	Mark Eccles, *Shakespeare in Warwickshire.*
Enc Brit	Encyclopedia Britannica, Vol. 4, 1988 ed.
Eng Hist Doc	*English Historical Documents, c. 500–1042,* ed. Dorothy Whitelock.
EKC	E. K. Chambers, *William Shakespeare: A Study of Facts and Problems,* 2 vols.

First Folio	*The First Folio of Shakespeare* (Facsimile), ed. Charlton Hinman.
Glanvill	Glanvill, *The treatise on the laws and customs of the realm of England commonly called Glanvill.*
Hist Eng Law	William Holdsworth, *A History of English Law,* 9 vols.
HLL	Dorothy Whitelock, *History, Law, and Literature in 10th–11th Century England.*
H-P, *Life*	James O. Halliwell (-Phillipps), *The Works of William Shakespeare,* Vol. I: *The Life of Shakespeare.*
H-P, *Life Abb*	———, *The Life of William Shakespeare Abbreviated.*
H-P, *Outlines*	———, *Outlines of the Life of Shakespeare.*
Lambarde	Wilbur Dunkel, *William Lambarde, Elizabethan Jurist, 1536–1601.*
Lincoln Wills	*Lincoln Wills,* Vol. 2: *A.D. 1505–May 1530,* ed. C. W. Foster.
Maitland	Frederic William Maitland, *English Law and the Renaissance.*
OED	*The Oxford English Dictionary.*
Pol & Mait	Sir Frederick Pollock and Frederic William Maitland, *The History of English Law before the Time of Edward I,* 3 vols.
Rec & Images	S. Schoenbaum, *William Shakespeare: Records and Images.*
Riverside Sh	*The Complete Works of Shakespeare,* ed. G. Blakemore Evans.
SEAALH	*Select Essays in Anglo-American Legal History,* 3 vols. (with author and title of each essay cited individually).
Shakesp Geneal	George Russell French, *Shakespeareanna Genealogica.*
Sh's Lives	S. Schoebaum, *Shakespeare's Lives.*
Sh/Pub Rec	*Shakespeare in the Public Records,* eds. David Thomas and Jane Cox.
Swinburne	Henry Swinburne, *A Briefe Treatise of Testaments and Last Willes* (1590, 1611, 1635).
Test Papers	E. Vine Hall, *Testamentary Papers II: Wills from Shakespeare's Town and Time.*
Will Med Eng	Michael Sheehan, *The Will in Medieval England: From the Conversion of the Anglo-Saxons to the End of the Thirteenth Century.*

Chapter One

The Will, Its Contents & the Controversies

"In the name of god Amen I William Shackspeare . . ."

Shakespeare's will comes down to us intact today largely because it has been carefully preserved on public display since at least 1737. According to George Vertue, who visited Stratford at that time, a copy was in the possession of Shakespeare Hart, descendant of the poet's sister, but the original was on display in Doctors' Commons,[1] a site of significance to my thesis in that it belonged to a society of lawyers in London forming a distinct profession for the practice of the civil and canon law (*Enc Brit* 145).[2] Thereafter, it was long preserved in Somerset House, London, until it was moved to the London Public Records Office Museum where it is now exhibited in a glass wall case.[3]

It is a three-page document, each page measuring approximately 12 inches by 15 inches, the second page alone numbered, all of it unparagraphed and unpunctuated, and many portions crossed through with emendations written in[4].

The interlineations, being the very last of the poet's public words so far as we know, are of great significance in that they represent the intimated gestures of the dying man. One interlineation in particular, that bequeathing the second best bed to his wife, has provoked many a critical scholar to commentary and interpretation. By recreating the contemporary contexts of meaning behind the legal transactions, we may the better interpret and discern Shakespeare's final concerns. Indeed, the poet's "last words" may have meant a good deal more to his wife than any bed could say.

However, before the major questions raised by the will can be elucidated, the contents of the will should be reviewed.

At this point I suggest the reader turn to the transcription of the will (Figure 1) and read it through. Seeing firsthand the rough form of the manuscript and having an overview of all the bequests will make it easier to follow the ensuing survey and analysis of the will's contents where I frequently allude to all the cancellations and interlineations.

The first of these appears at the top of the very first page, where two dates are written in: "Vicesimo Quinto die Januarii" (January 25) with only the month cancelled out and "Martii" (March) written above it. It is from just such changes as these that disputes have arisen, so the reader will find it most helpful to gain some familiarity with the original before embarking on the survey which follows.

THE CONTENTS OF THE WILL

In summary, apart from a few specific items such as his sword and clothing, all the real property, that is, houses and lands, was bequeathed to the poet's elder daughter, Susanna Shakespeare Hall, and entailed upon her eldest son or male heirs. Cash bequests totalled a value of £350,[5] with most of the money entailed in the legacy for the other surviving daughter, Judith (Shakespeare's only son, her twin, having died at an early age).

The will is framed into ten distinct "Items." Most of the first page is taken up with Judith's bequest, largely as a result of her hasty marriage to Thomas Quiney, which took place on February 10, between the dates of the first draft (January 25, presumably) and the second one (presumably March 25). Thus, the first Item is: "I Gyve & bequeath vnto my [sonne in L] daughter Judyth One Hundred & ffyftie poundes" (brackets denote cancellations).

The £100 was *"in discharge of her marriage porcion"* (italics denote interlineations), and the remaining £50 was contingent upon her surrender of claim to the manor of Rowington, the Cottage in Chapel Lane. This required a family settlement which was acted upon the following year (see Chapter Two). In the second Item she is granted even more, £150, if she or any child were still living after three years, and for as long as she was married the interest from this sum was to be paid her, though not the principal. In order to receive the initial £150, her husband had to settle lands of the same value on her and her children. In the event that Judith or a child were *not* living, the sum was to be divided between Elizabeth Hall, Shakespeare's granddaughter (confusingly referred to in the Will as his "Neece," a point the reader will find explained in a later section dealing with legal terminology), daughter of Susanna and her husband, John Hall, then only eight years old,[6] who would get £100, and his sister, Joan Hart, or her children, who would receive £50 "to be sett fourth by my executours. . . ." Judith's "marriage porcion" amounted to a contract with Quiney for the protection of Judith's and her children's future, a proviso reinforced by the interlineated words *"by my executours & overseers* for the best benefitt of her & her issue. . . ." In addition to her "marriage porcion," Shakespeare also gave to Judith his "brod silver & gilt bole," a specific provision which had been cited in the original draft as well.

The third Item is the bequest to his sister, Joan Hart, then forty-seven years old. To her he bequeathed £20 and all his wearing apparel, probably because he assumed that either her husband, William Hart, the hatter, or her three sons would have need of male attire, not knowing at the time the will was being drawn up that his brother-in-law would be buried on April 17, one week before his own death. He also gave his sister life tenancy in the house in which she and her family were living, Henley House, (Figure 2) his father's home where he and she may (or may not) have been born but where they certainly spent their childhood.[7] Item 4 refers to her three sons (aged sixteen, eleven, and eight) to whom he left £5 apiece. Apparently, Shakespeare recalled the names of William, the eldest, and Michael, the youngest, but not that of Thomas, the middle one, a fact that led James O. Halliwell-Phillipps to conclude that there must have been great haste in devising the will since the Christian name of Shakespeare's own nephew was omitted (H-P, *Life* 2:244).[8] It is of some interest that this boy was at the time the same age as Shakespeare's own son, Hamnet, upon his death on August 11, 1596.

This bequest to his nephews takes up the first two lines on the second page. It was recorded high on the page above three cancelled lines remaining from the original draft, a section pertaining to Judith. The content of these three lines confirms the theory that it was indeed her marriage that necessitated the redrafting: "[to be sett out for her within one Yeare after my deceas by my executours with thadvise and direccions of my overseers for her best proffitt vntill her Marriage and then the same with the increase thereof to be paied vnto her] Item I gyve & bequeath unto [her] *the saied Elizabeth Hall* All my plate. . . ." Originally, therefore, Shakespeare may have intended Judith to have all the

Figure 1 Shakespeare's Will. A transcription with line endings and punctuation corresponding to the original. Words printed in italics and on separate lines are interlineations in the original. Words lined through are cancelled in the original.

Martii

Vicesimo Quinto die ~~Januarii~~ Anno Regni Domini nostri Jacobi nunc Regis Anglie
&c decimo quarto & Scotie xlix^{o} Annoque domini 1616

T[estamentum] W[illel]^{mj} Shackspeare

In the name of god Amen I William Shackspeare of Stratford vpon Avon in the countie
of Warr gent in perfect health & memorie god be praysed doe make & Ordayne this
my last will & testament in manner & forme followeing That ys to saye ffirst I Comend
my Soule into the handes of god my Creator hoping & assuredlie beleeving through
thonelie merittes of Jesus Christe my Saviour to be made partaker of lyfe everlastinge
And my bodye to the Earth whereof yt ys made Item I Gyve & bequeath
vnto my ~~sonne in L~~ daughter Judyth One Hundred & ffyftie poundes of lawfull
English money to be paied vnto her in manner & forme followeing that ys to

in discharge of her marriage porcion

saye One Hundred Poundes^within one yeare after my deceas with consideracion
after the Rate of twoe shillinges in the pound for soe long tyme as the same
shalbe vnpaied vnto her after my deceas & the ffyftie poundes Residewe thereof

of

vpon her Surrendring^or gyving of such sufficient securitie as the overseers of
this my will shall like of to Surrender or graunte All her estate & Right that

that shee

shall discend or come vnto her after my deceas or^nowe hath of in or to one
Copiehold tenemente with thappurtenaunces lyeing & being in Stratford vpon Avon
aforesaied in the saied countie of Warr being parcell or holden of the mannour of
Rowington vnto my daughter Susanna Hall & her heires for ever
Item I Gyve & bequeath unto my saied daughter Judith One

Hundred & ffyftie Poundes more if shee or Anie issue of her bodie be
Lyvinge att thend of three Yeares next ensueing the daie of the date
of this my will during which tyme my executours to paie her consideracion from
my deceas according to the Rate aforesaied And if she dye within the saied
terme without issue of her bodye then my will ys & I doe gyve & bequeath
One Hundred Poundes thereof to my Neece Elizabeth Hall & the ffiftie
Poundes to be sett fourth by my executours during the lief of my Sister
Johane Harte & the vse & proffitt thereof Cominge shalbe payed to my saied
Sister Jone & after her deceas the saied l[li] shall Remaine Amongst the
children of my saied Sister Equallie to be devided Amongst them But
if my saied daughter Judith be lyving att thend of the saied three Yeares or
anie yssue of her bodye then my will ys & soe I devise & bequeath the

by my executours & overseers

saied Hundred and ffyftie poundes to be sett out for the best benefitt of her & her

the stock to be

issue & not paied unto her soe long as she shalbe marryed & covert Baron
~~by my executours & overseers~~ but my will ys that she shall have the consideracion
yearelie paied vnto her during her lief & after her deceas the saied stock and
consideracion to bee paied to her children if she have Anie & if not to her
executours or assignes she lyving the saied terme after my deceas provided that yf
such husbond as she shall att thend of the saied three Yeares be marryed vnto or attaine
after doe sufficientlie Assure vnto her & thissue of her bodie landes Awnswereable to
the porcion by this my will gyven vnto her & to be adiudged soe by my executours
& overseers then my will ys that the saied cl[li] shalbe paied to such husbond as
shall make such assurance to his owne vse Item I gyve and bequeath vnto my saied
sister Jone xx[li] and all my wearing Apparrell to be paied & delivered within one yeare

the house

after my deceas And I doe will&devise vnto her with thappurtenaunces in Stratford wherein
she dwelleth for her naturall lief vnder the yearelie Rent of xij[d] Item I gyve and bequeath

William Shakspere

vnto her three sonns Welliam Harte . . . Hart & Michaell Harte
ffyve poundes A peece to be payed within one Yeare after my deceas
~~to be sett out for her within one Yeare after my deceas by my executours~~
~~with thadvise and direccions of my overseers for her best proffitt vntill her~~
~~Marriage and then the same with the increase thereof to be paied~~ vnto

the saied Elizabeth Hall except my brod silver & gilt bole

~~her~~ Item I gyve & bequeath vnto ~~her~~ All my Plate that I now
have att the date of this my will Item I gyve & bequeath vnto
the Poore of Stratford aforesaied tenn poundes to mr Thomas
Combe my Sword to Thomas Russell Esquier ffyve poundes &
to ffrauncis Collins of the Borough of Warr in the countie of Warr
gent thirteene poundes Sixe shillinges & Eight pence to be paied within

Hamlett Sadler

one Yeare after my deceas Item I gyve & bequeath to ~~mr Richard~~

to William Raynoldes gent xxvj^{s} viij^{d} to buy him A Ringe

~~Tyler thelder~~ xxvj^{s} viij^{d} to buy him A Ringe to my godson William
Walker xx^{s} in gold to Anthonye Nashe gent xxvj^{s} viij^{d} & to Mr

& to my ffellowes John Hemynge Richard Burbage & Henry Cundell

viij^{d} xxvj^{s} viij^{d} A peece to buy them Ringes

John Nashe xxvj^{s} ~~in gold~~ Item I Gyve Will bequeath & Devise vnto

for better enabling of her to performe this my will & towardes the performans thereof

my daughter Susanna Hall All that Capitall Messuage or tenemente

in Stratford aforesaied

with thappurtenaunces Called the new place wherein I nowe dwell

& twoe messuages or tenementes withappurtenaunces scituat lyeing and being
in Henley streete within the borough of Stratford aforesaied And all
my barnes stables Orchardes gardens landes tenementes & hereditamentes whatsoever

scituat lyeing & being or to be had Receyved perceyved or taken
within the townes Hamlettes villages ffieldes & groundes of Stratford
vpon Avon Oldstratford Bushopton & Welcombe or in anie of them
in the saied countie of Warr And alsoe All that Messuage or
tenemente with thappurtennaunces wherein one John Robinson dwelleth scituat
lyeing & being in the blackfriers in London nere the Wardrobe & all
other my landes tenementes & hereditamentes whatsoever To Have & to hold All &
singuler the saied premisses with their Appurtennaunces vnto the saied Susanna
Hall for & during the terme of her naturall lief & after her
Deceas to the first sonne of her bodie lawfullie yssueing & to the
heires Males of the bodie of the saied first Sonne lawfullie
yssueinge & for defalt of such issue to the second Sonne of her
bodie lawfullie issueinge & to the heires Males of the bodie of the
saied Second Sonne lawfullie yssueinge & for defalt of such
heires to the third Sonne of the bodie of the saied Susanna
Lawfullie yssueing & of the heires Males of the bodie of the saied third
sonne lawfullie yssueing And for defalt of such issue the same soe
to be & Remaine to the ffourth ~~sonne~~ ffyfth sixte & Seaventh
sonnes of her bodie lawfullie issueing one after Another & to the heires

Willm Shakspere

Males of the bodies of the saied fourth fifth Sixte & Seaventh sonnes
lawfullie yssueing in such manner as yt ys before Lymitted to be & Remaine
to the first second & third Sonns of her bodie & to their heires Males
And for defalt of such issue the saied premisses to be & Remaine to my
sayed Neece Hall & the heires males of her bodie Lawfullie
yssueing & for defalt of such issue to my daughter Judith
& the heires Males of her bodie lawfullie yssueinge And for
defalt of such issue to the Right heires of me the saied William
Item I gyve unto my wief my second best bed with the furniture
Shackspere for ever ^ Item I gyve & bequeath to my saied daughter
Judith my broad silver gilt bole All the Rest of my goodes Chattels
Leases plate Jewels & householde stuffe whatsoever after my dettes and
legasies paied & my funerall expences discharged I gyve devise
& bequeath to my Sonne in Lawe John Hall gent & my daughter
Susanna his wief whom I ordaine & make executours of this my
the saied
Last will & testament And I doe intreat & Appoint ^ Thomas
Russell Esquier & ffrauncis Collins gent to be overseers hereof And
doe Revoke All former wills & publishe this to be my last

will & testament In witnesse whereof I have hereunto put my
hand
~~seale~~ the daie & Yeare first aboue Written

By me William Shakspeare

witnes to the publishing
hereof Fra: Collyns
Julyus Shawe
John Robinson
Hamnet Sadler
Robert Whattcott

Probatum coram magistro Willielmo Byrde legum doctore
commissario &c xxij[do] die mensis Junii Anno domini 1616
Juramento Johannis Hall vnius executoris &c Cui &c
de bene &c Jurato Reservata potestate &c Susanne Hall
alteri executori &c cum venerit &c petitura Inventorium exhibitum

Figure 2 The Birthplace Today.

plate but in the revision of the fifth Item gives it instead to his granddaughter; the words *"except my brod silver & gilt bole"* are interlineated, followed by the original wording "that I now have at the date of this my will." The interlineations from this point on are taken by Halliwell-Phillipps to be "the testimonies we may cherish of his last faltering accents to the world he was leaving" (H-P, *Life* 2:244).

Items 6 and 7 differ from the others in citing a cluster of bequests instead of denoting only one. In Item 6 there are four specific bequests: "tenn poundes" to the poor of Stratford, quite a generous sum for this traditional legacy, usually £2 or less; his sword to Thomas Combe, youngest son of Thomas Combe, Sr., and nephew and heir of John Combe, the richest man in Stratford. John Combe had been Shakespeare's lifelong friend; he had known the poet's parents, John and Mary Shakespeare, and the Nash family into which Shakespeare's granddaughter eventually married.[9] Not having any living son of his own to whom he might leave his sword, Shakespeare left it to the heir of his best friend. To the two overseers of his will, he left £5 to Thomas Russell "Esquier" and to Francis Collins of the borough of Warwick in the county of Warwickshire, "gent," £13 6*s*. 8*d*.., "to be paied within one Yeare after my decease."

Following this in Item 7 are the interlineated bequests to two friends, *"Hamlett Sadler"* and *"William Raynoldes gent.,"* of 26*s*. 8*d*. each for memorial rings. Sadler, a High Street baker who had stood godfather to Shakespeare's son in 1585 before the playwright left Stratford, was also a witness to the will. His name was "Hamnet," yet here it is given as "Hamlett" (H-P, *Life* 2:244). Raynoldes, or Reynolds, was a connection by marriage of the Combe family, according to Robert Speaight,[10] and neighbor of Shakespeare's father on Henley Street in 1552 (H-P, *Life* 2:245). When their names were added in the late alteration, Sadler's name replaced that of Mr. Richard Tyler the elder, who in the original draft had been the first cited as recipient of such a ring.

The next legatee included in Item 7, cited in the original will as well, was Shakespeare's own godson, William Walker, son of Henry Walker, alderman, bailiff, prominent man of Stratford (Speaight 206). Peter Levi tells us William "was baptized on 16 October 1608, so he was only seven years old" (342).[11] William was given twenty shillings in gold. In the following two bequests, "to Anthonye Nashe gent," and "Mr. John Nashe" (future father and uncle, respectively, of Thomas, who later married Shakespeare's granddaughter, Elizabeth Hall) he left 26*s*. 8*d*. for a ring, "in gold" crossed out. Following this is the interlineation *"& to my ffellowes John Hemynge Richard Burbage & Henry Cundell,"* all fellows of the King's Men acting troupe, the same amount, *"A peece to buy them Ringes."* Heminges and Condell, well known as editors of the First Folio in 1623, were also churchwardens at St. Mary Aldermanbury in London and directed activities of the King's Men (BRL 2:488).

Item 8, the longest of the bequests, pertains to Susanna Hall. To the original legal formula "I Gyve Will bequeath & Devise" was added *"for better enabling of her to performe this my will & towardes the performans thereof. . . ."* To her he left "All that Capitall Messuage or tenemente with thappurtenaunces *in Stratford aforesaied* Called the newe place wherein I nowe dwell & twoe messuages or tenementes . . . scituat lyeing and being in Henley streete. . . . And all my barnes stables Orchardes gardens landes tenementes & hereditamentes . . . within . . . Stratford vpon Avon Oldstratford Bushopton & Welcombe. . . ." (see Figure 3). He also left her the property "in the blackfriers in London" which was let to one John Robinson, to be held entail to her male heirs "lawfullie yssueing" even to the "Seaventh sonnes" and their "heires males," or in default of these to Elizabeth Hall "& the heires males of

Figure 3 The Site of New Place Today.

her bodie,'' or in default of such issue, to Judith and her ''heires Males,'' and in default of such issue ''to the Right heires of me the saied William Shackspere for ever.''

In the original draft the bequest to Judith of the ''broad [sic] silver gilt bole'' immediately followed this bequest to her sister. But in the final draft, between this lengthy one to Susanna Hall and the very specific one to Judith, appears Item 9, the interlineation of the notorious remembrance to his wife: *''Item I gyve unto my wief my second best bed with the furniture.''* Thus, at this point in the will, at the end of establishing the succession of all their issue, specific family bequests begin with this one to his wife, followed by that of the bowl to Judith in Item 10 and finally the remainder to the Halls.

The remainder of ''goodes Chattels Leases plate Jewels & householde stuffe,'' after all debts and legacies are paid and funeral expenses discharged, are left ''to my Sonne in Lawe John Hall gent & my daughter Susanna his wief whom I ordaine & make executours of this my Last will & testament.'' He entreated and appointed Thomas Russell and Francis Collins to be overseers. ''In witnesse whereof I have hereunto put my [seale] *hand* the daie & Yeare first aboue Written.'' The final alteration was this cancellation of ''seale'' and addition of ''hand.''

At the end it is signed "By me William Shakspeare"—on the first two pages the signature appended at the bottom of each page appears as "William Shakspere" and "Willm Shakspere, respectively (Eccles 142)—followed by the names of the witnesses: Francis Collins, solicitor residing in Warwick, who may have drawn up the will and who was to become town clerk of Stratford by 1616 (died 1617); July or Julius Shaw, who lived two doors from New Place (H-P, *Life* 2:245) and who was high bailiff of Stratford (the post once held by John Shakespeare) and an alderman as well; John Robinson, possibly the one who was renting from Shakespeare the Blackfriars property in London at this time (but there were several John Robinsons in Stratford at the time, one a laborer);[12] Hamnet Sadler; and Robert Whattcott. In fact, Robinson and Whattcott are now thought to have been servants of either Shakespeare or the Halls. Records show that Whattcott testified for, or may have been attorney for, Susanna Hall in a Consistory Court case of 1613 in which she had to appear for defamation of character (EKC 2:178). In any event, from a record of Chancery Court, cited by Frank Marcham in *William Shakespeare and His Daughter Susannah,* Shakespeare's last surviving descendant, his granddaughter Elizabeth Hall, lived at New Place after her father's death in 1635 with her mother and husband Thomas Nash, until his death in 1647. In 1649 she was married again, to John Bernard, later Sir John Bernard.[13] They continued to live at New Place until 1653, when they moved to his family estate at Abingdon, where she died in February 1670, bequeathing New Place outside the Shakespeare family (Bentley 68–9).

An inventory of Shakespeare's goods was attached to the will and was taken into court with it, but it has never been found.[14]

THE CONTROVERSIES

Of all the documents related to Shakespeare this one has been the object of peculiarly avid curiosity and controversy—its three pages assiduously studied, each nuance and ink mark pondered and speculated upon, the meaning of obscurities vigorously contested. Why was the first page redrafted and the date altered? Why the unusual number of witnesses? Why the preponderance of bequests to his children, in particular to the elder daughter? And most belabored of all, in what S. Schoenbaum alludes to as "arguably the most notorious bequest in literary history" (*Sh's Lives* 145), why the "second best bed" to his wife?

All the controversy over Shakespeare's will has proven invaluable, of course, in prompting the extensive and highly specialized scholarship that today brings us whatever understanding we do have regarding these so-called problematical elements of the will. The primary reason for what Robert Speaight calls the ''needlessly heavy weather'' (371) made over the will itself in general and the ''notorious'' bequest in particular is that a will is taken as a measure of the testator's relationships to those he or she remembers in his or her last days. As Professor Schoenbaum judiciously observes, the will ''does yield a glimpse of Shakespeare's purpose in building an estate from proceeds of his play-writing, and it enshrines the names of those he cherished most in Stratford and London'' (*Doc Life* 246).

Indeed, what the poet left to others was a subject of gossip early on if John Aubrey's entry in *Brief Lives* is any indication: ''I thinke I have been told that he left 2 or 300 pounds per annum there and thereabouts to a sister.''[15] But the gossip was not always of such a simple nature. From Shakespeare's will, inferences have been made impugning both Anne Hathaway Shakespeare's character (e.g., there is ''nothing to indicate wit, or education, or anything but a housewife keeping house for the errant player who chose life in London'') and their marriage (''The utter silence about Shakespeare's wife is some indication of her place in the scheme of things—a housewife, and nothing more'').[16] Inferences in this vein have stirred up strong reactions, like that of William Dean Howells, who in *The Seen and Unseen at Stratford-on-Avon: A Fantasy* confesses to Shakespeare's ''ghost,'' ''The worst grudge I ever had against you was because of that second-best bed.''[17]

The negative surmisings have been countered by others of a complimentary, occasionally even sentimental, nature such as that of Speaight—that the '' 'best' bed was normally reserved for guests'' and that what Shakespeare left to his wife was the conjugal bed, ''the four-poster in which they had slept together, albeit intermittently, at least from the time of their establishment at New Place'' (371). Such theories, even the most ingenious among them, are at best, as Edward Wagenknecht has pointed out, ''sheer hypothesis.''[18]

Disputation over the will was not always concerned with bequests only. Among the first aspects targeted for criticism were its form and style. Nicholas Rowe, the first modern editor of Shakespeare, represents the view of those who have found the form somewhat disappointing: in 1709 he dismissed the matter by declaring that ''the spirit of the man is to be found in his works.''[19] A similar tone of embarrassment appears in the description given by the Reverend Joseph Greene, the Stratford antiquary, master of the local grammar school, and vicar of Holy Trinity Church, where Shakespeare was buried, who found the will in 1747 and made a transcript of it for the first person to show interest in it, a Mr. West of Abscot. Indeed, the Rev. Greene thought the ''only satisfaction'' one might have in reading the will ''is to know who were his Relations, and what he left them, which perhaps may just make you also amends for ye trouble of perusing it.''[20]

> The Legaicies and Bequests therein . . . are undoubtedly as he intended; but the manner of introducing them, appears to me so dull and irregular, so absolutely void of y least particle of that Spirit which Animated Our great Poet; that it must lessen his Character as a Writer, to imagine y least Sentence of it his production.(59)

At the other extreme, scholars of our own time accept the lackluster quality of the style as being simply a feature of ''a characteristic will of a man of property in the reign of James I.''[21]

I agree with the Reverend Greene that ''ye trouble of perusing it'' is rewarded by knowing more about his ''Relations'' and friends and what he left them. The old idea that the second best bed is derogatory is exploded now, and other matters are more or less acceptably explained. But there are other rewards to be gained from studying the poet's testament, as I will show in the following elucidation of the major questions raised by it. Legal documents of the time provide conclusive evidence for a reassessment of the document, both as an instrument of sound legal strategy and poignant personal testimony.

THE MANUSCRIPT

Questions arise, first, as to the very condition of the manuscript itself. The corrections, deletions, interlineations—who made them and why were they made? Do they provide clues to circumstances surrounding his death? Moreover, some of them introduce curious bequests by today's standards. Was there some particular importance or meaning ascribed to them at the time?

It has been argued that Shakespeare himself penned the will in his ''legal hand.'' E. B. Everitt, for example, following the ''young noverint'' tradition dating from Chalmers and Malone in the eighteenth century, which claimed that Shakespeare had gained legal knowledge during the 1580s serving as a scrivener or *noverint,* concludes that

Shakespeare himself penned the will.[22] Charles Hamilton, too, considers the entire will holographic (6) and explains that the blunders and "carelessness and hesitation in the mode of expression" (75) are the result of an attempt on the poet's life during the actual time of the will's devisement. Certainly we should assume there is some plausible reason, though perhaps nothing so extraordinary as a murder plot, which would account for the many blots and changes, if the will were indeed written by one who, we are told by his friends Heminges and Condell, "vttered with that easinesse, that wee have scarse receiued from him a blot in his papers" (*First Folio* 7).

Although it is known that Francis Collins was the solicitor Shakespeare called upon to devise the will, the consensus of opinion is that he himself did not write it. Even though the document does bear the telling signs of being unparagraphed and unpunctuated that were Collins's usual practice, in the opinion of N. E. Nash presented by Schoenbaum, the handwriting in which the will was drawn up differs considerably from specimens of Collins's hand in other documents (*Doc Life* 242). The will could also have been written out by Collins's clerk or scrivener. The issue is by no means settled. Eccles for one asserts unequivocally that the handwriting "matches exactly his [Collins's] handwriting in the Council Book" (119–20).

The manuscript is curious in still another regard: the first page has few interlineations, while page 2 has extensive ones and page 3 only one significant one and two minor ones. Furthermore, at the top of page 2 is a canceled passage that would have made no sense in connection with the existing page 1, but the two lines now added above this section do form a continuation from the bottom line of page 1, which, incidentally, was written in more crowded script very far down into the margin as if to allow for preservation of the original page 2.

Thus it would appear that although the marked-through date at the upper right of the first page indicates a prior devisement, only the first page was completely redone. The other two sheets remain to this day, bearing for all to see the many changes and additions requested by the testator. In the *Compact Documentary Life* Schoenbaum presents the situation as one in which the "lawyer took down the dying man's words," Shakespeare catching himself at certain points, "Collins (or his clerk)" then crossing out words and making necessary changes (299). *March* 25, 1616, the date of the second draft, was probably the day the lawyer came to New Place where Shakespeare was presumably lying ill (*Doc Life* 246). This supposition is supported by the fact that the major changes in the will are those pertaining to Judith, whose marriage took place after the January date and before the March one, on February 10. Judith's marriage does seem to have made it necessary for him to provide a marriage *portion* instead of the marriage *dowry* that evidence indicates was provided originally. B. Roland Lewis thinks "that Shakespeare had provided such a marriage dowry in the earlier sheet 1" since "the deleted three lines . . . mention this very item, at the top of sheet 2 of the will (the cancelled passage)" (BRL 2:472).

Other events also must have fueled the change of the bequest to Judith as Hugh A. Hanley discovered in the Act book of the Stratford Vicar's Court, which he found in 1964 among the papers of a family in Maidstone, Kent.[23] From Hanley we find out that Thomas Quiney, Judith's fiancé, was brought to trial for having conceived a child out of wedlock with another woman nine months prior to the time of his engagement and subsequent marriage to Judith Shakespeare (Hanley 441). The volatility of this situation cannot be underestimated, nor can its effects upon the Shakespeare family at the time. Quiney's trial was set for March 26; the will was altered the day before, on March 25. Ten days earlier, on March 15, the burials of both mother and baby had been recorded in the Stratford register. Quiney's public penance was to appear clothed in a sheet, the custom of the time, for three Sundays in the church of Stratford. But he paid 5 shillings, requested penance be remitted and was subsequently dismissed (Hanley 441).

In addition to this already scandalous situation, and no doubt a source of further stress for the Shakespeare family, Thomas and Judith were called to appear before an ecclesiastical court because their February 10 marriage was declared out of season. According to ecclesiastical court law of that day, certain seasons were restricted. Calculations made by Rudstone, a noted calendarist of the time, in his section on the Lenten season, are representative: "Times prohibited from marriage is from December the 2, to January the 1. Againe, from January the 29 to Aprill the 7, also from May the 5, to the 25, of May."[24] In Quiney's defense, there is evidence that he did obtain a license for their marriage, but because of a dispute between the Bishop's court and the Vicar's Court, it was not properly recorded, for which, as Hanley puts it, "he could hardly be held responsible by Shakespeare" (Hanley 441). Of course, it may also have been that they had no choice but to marry out of season, since a son was born to them only seven months later, in September. Sometime between February 10 and May 11, after having been twice summoned, Quiney and Judith were given the sentence of excommunication, but this did not prevent their son, Shakespeare Quiney, from being baptized in the church.

Similarly, with regard to the interlineations one must proceed with care. The common assumption is that any bequest that was merely interlineated must therefore have been only an afterthought. Charles Elton, an experienced real property lawyer, points out that this is not necessarily the case: "Yet interlineation does seem to give the bequest a special emphasis since these must have been the very last words, added to express the final emendations to the will."[25] The kinds of things interlineated were the bequests to Burbage, Heminges and Condell, Hamlet Sadler, and of course the "notorious" one to his wife.

It is the opinion of Professor Lewis that there is really no way of proving that the will's interlineations were added in March and that they were perhaps even "inserted at the time those sheets were first written" (BRL 2:474 and see Eccles 141).

Examination of the original will, however, leads me to question the supposition that all the pages were written on the same day, for even to the naked eye the ink appears quite noticeably darker on the entire first page, as well as in all the changes made on subsequent pages and in the signatures of the witnesses, than it does in the body of pages 2 and 3.[26] Only Collins's signature is in the same lighter tint as the other body material on page 3.

The two kinds of ink would certainly suggest two ink bottles. The body of the will could have been done in another place and only the interlining from Shakespeare's dictation, using Shakespeare's ink. However, this would not explain the changes on page 2, which clearly indicate an earlier draft. Moreover, it seems highly unlikely that the scrivener would mistake the month of March for January. The date itself was not changed, an indication that the solicitor (scrivener) began by merely copying from the original page, then caught himself and changed the month to the later one of the alteration. The ink in which the new month was written is in the same darker tint as that of the entire new page.

All of this suggests that the first page and the alterations, but not all three pages, were made at the same time. However, decisive proof must be deferred to the discussion of forms of testaments, because the retention of pages 2 and 3 may have been deliberate in order to ensure the will's compliance with a legal stipulation assigned to a particular kind of testament. Even the minute detail of "Martii" marked over "Januarii" could have great impact upon the legal ramifications of the will, as we learn from the immensely valuable work of Henry Swinburne, acknowledged by Schoenbaum as being "our authority of last resort on Elizabethan wills" (*Rec & Images* 98), namely *A Briefe Treatise of Testaments and Last Willes*.[27] It was a sourcebook that would have been known to Shakespeare as Jane Cox assures us that he was "almost certainly familiar with the works of Henry Swinburne" (*Sh/Pub Rec* 24).[28]

In Swinburne's treatise, to be examined in the following chapter, we find a full account of those things that pertain to the "general internall forme" of a will and testament, as well as those things pertaining to the "generall externall forme." Indeed, this civil testamentary law sourcebook provides the resolutions to many points of controversy in Shakespeare's will.

Chapter Two

The Will as Solemn Testament

> "Wills . . . and testaments, rights of inheritance and successions, are all of them creatures of the civil or municipal laws, and accordingly are in all respects regulated by them."
>
> —Blackstone, *Commentaries,* 2:12.

Swinburne's *A Briefe Treatise of Testaments and Last Willes* shows that Shakespeare's will precisely follows the testamentary laws of his day. From this manual on the devisement of a legal will, we shall (1) determine the kind of will Shakespeare's is; (2) compare the requisites of that testamentary form to the controversial aspects in Shakespeare's will; and (3) examine a special legal privilege attached to this testamentary form that both accounts for the preponderance of bequests to the children and guarantees the incontestability of the document. We shall discover a legal reason for the naming of an executor as well as obtain answers for other questions that have arisen over certain aspects of the poet's will. In particular, the testamentary document called the Solemn Testament must be considered at length because of the several parallels one finds between it and the controversial aspects of Shakespeare's will noted in the previous chapter, namely, the unusual number of witnesses, the signatures, and specific alterations.

Swinburne accounts for all of these points and incidentally even confirms the fact that the document's rough form would in no way invalidate it. The testament of any man "may be revoked or altered at any time and as oft as the Testator will, whiles he liveth, even untill his last breath; and of these the last shall prevaileth" (Swinburne 1611, 8^{V} [the page is out of order, coming before 9]; 1590, fol. 9, no signature but C4 on 8, no signatures then until 5 pages later at D13).

WILLS AND TESTAMENTS

Swinburne makes it absolutely clear that while all testaments are wills, not all wills are testaments. The distinction lies in the naming of an executor. "It is the naming or appointment of an Executor (who in the Civill law is called Haeres heire) . . . by the which onely the will is made a Testament" (Swinburne 1611, 7^V / C7^V; 1590, 7^V / C3). In Shakespeare's case the naming of Susanna and John Hall follows the most direct form: the assignation is "pure and simple, when the Testator maketh his Executor without any condition, as if the Testator say, I make A. B. my executor or thus, I will that A. B. be my executor" (Swinburne 1611, 129^V–130 / T3^V–T4; 1590, 117–117^V / R–R^V). The testament had also to have the character of a *sentence,* that is, "an advised purpose, or destination of the Testator's minde . . . representing as it were the persons of grave men, and of iust Judges" (Swinburne 1611 7^V–9 [pages out of order] / C7^V–C8; 1590, 7^V–8 / C3–C3^V).
Swinburne adds:

> And certainely if all the actions of this life ought to be performed with wisedome, and constancie; if nothing ought to be attempted without carefull consideration, and due premeditation: how much more ought the last act of our life, our farewell to the world, the memoriall of our immortality, even our testaments and last wils, to be framed with deliberation, seasoned with discretion, and builded upon and sound and constant determination: without the which it hath neither shape, nor savour, of a testament; nor is able to stand for a testament, when it shall be tried or prooved in the forme of Law? (Swinburne 1611, 9 / C8; 1590, 8–8^V / C4–C4^V)

For legality both a testament and a will depended upon certain proofs:

> Wherefore + that willes and testaments may Lawfully appeare, it is requisite that there bee sufficient proofe, either by *witnesse,* or by *writing.* (Swinburne 1611, 205 / Ee7; 1590, 185^V / Bb5^V)

Shakespeare's will is therefore indisputably a testament in that it both names an executor (two, in fact) and is clearly a statement which one can reasonably assume reflects the testator's purpose in devisement. Moreover, its legality is unquestionable since it fulfills both requirements for sufficient proof, namely, witness and writing. In fact, there were more witnesses than were necessary for the will to have been simply legal.

Halliwell-Phillipps was the first to call attention to the "unusual" number of witnesses.[1] Since then various explanations have been given. B. Roland Lewis sums up the representative notions: (1) that since Collins and Sadler were beneficiaries, "three others were called in so as to be certain to make the will valid"; (2) that "since the will was a hurried, rough draft, only a plentiful supply of witnesses could make it valid"; and (3) that "Collins alone witnessed the first complete draft and that when on March 25, 1616, the first page was redrafted and rewritten, the additional four witnesses were hastily called in as further attesters" (BRL 2:493). E. K. Chambers thought that Collins was careful to secure five witnesses since two of them were legatees "whose legacies would be invalidated if they had to give testimony" (BRL 2:177). Yet, still another explanation is simply that it wasn't all that uncommon a number, as Mark Eccles posits, for five witnesses had also been named in the will of Shakespeare's grandfather, Robert Arden (Eccles 142).

What does Swinburne say about the number of witnesses? Two witnesses alone were "needfull" and "sufficient," *if* they be "without cause of exception." He adds:

> But what if the witnesses bee not free from all exception, but yet are more in number then two, suppose three or foure: whether be they sufficient for proofe of the Will? It may bee answered, that if the exceptions whereunto the witnesses are subject, be light or slender, such as do in part diminish the credite of their Testimony, as the exception of friendship, domesticie, or of suspition of some small fault, there the number doth supply the defect, & so the testimonie of three witnesses, not altogether clear from those exceptions, is as the Testimonie of two witnesses, without all exception. (Swinburne 1611, 206 / Ee8; 1590, 186 / no signature until 189 = C [185 = Bb5])

Neither kindred nor tenants nor servants could serve as witnesses; therefore, it is unlikely that the witness John Robinson was John Robinson tenant of Blackfriars (Swinburne 1611, 207 / Ff; 1590, 187 / no signature). As to the testimony of a legatee, such as Francis Collins, Hamnet Sadler, or Thomas Russell, all of whom were named beneficiaries in the will, his witness was considered "good for the rest of the Will, but not for his owne Legacy" (Swinburne 1611, 207^{V} / Ff^{V}; 1590, 187^{V} / no signature).

So the unusual number of witnesses to Shakespeare's will can be accounted for as compensation either for legatees' claims or for the "lighter" exception due to friendship. A further explanation provides a key to several other points as well, namely: (1) why all three sheets of the will bear Shakespeare's signature, (2) why only the first page was corrected and affixed to the former two, and (3) why Shakespeare's children instead of his wife are the principal beneficiaries. Indeed, there are several peculiarities to the testament that identify it as having been as distinct a *kind* of testament as the testament was a distinctive kind of will.

THE SOLEMN TESTAMENT

There were two kinds of testaments, the solemn and the unsolemn. Apparently one of the many confusing issues in Swinburne's day arose from the authority of common law over Roman civil law, especially with regard to the form of testaments, whether solemn or unsolemn. The Solemn Testament, based upon the Roman civil law from Justinian, called for seven witnesses, "whereof," writes Swinburne, "the Romane people were strictly tyed, in the making of their Testaments. . . . so that if any one of these solemnities were omitted, the Testament was void" (1611, 19^{V}–20 / $E2^{V}$–E3; 1590, 17–18 / no signature [16 is D4 and 21 is E]). Swinburne carefully and repeatedly points out of Solemn Testaments that "no man is necessarily tied thereunto heere in England," the Justinian codes having been "reformed first by the Ecclesiasticall Law, which did reduce the number of seven witnesses to three (the parochiall minister being one) and in some cases two; and then by the generall custome of this Realme, which distinctly requireth no mo witnesses then two, so they be free from any iust cause of exception" (Swinburne 1611, 20 / E3; 1590, 17–17^{V} / no signature).

Thus all testaments in England at this time were regarded in the strict sense as *Unsolemn Testaments,* as Swinburne acknowledged:

> *Unsolemne Testaments* are so termed, whereas the solemnities of the Civill law above mentioned, or any of them are omitted, at the making of the Testament: without the which by the Civill Law, the Testaments were voyde except in certaine cases. But with us in *England* they are not void: for that our Testaments are not subject to the ceremonies of the Civill Law, but are made with all liberty and freedome. . . . How doth the definition of a Testament above mentioned, borrowed out of the Civill

> Law, agree with our Testaments here in *England,* being all unsolemne Testaments?

However, in spite of the autonomous validity of the English testament as unsolemn, Swinburne still recognizes a differentiation between two kinds of testaments in terms of solemnities:

> It should seeme we had need to seeke a new definition, and that I have erred, together with other our Common and temporall Lawyers of this Realme, in borrowing that definition, which agreeth so just with their Testaments, with which Testaments our Testaments doe not agree. . . . My opinion is this, that the definition doth comprehend, both *solemne* and *unsolemne Testaments* and therefore is agreeable to our Testaments. . . . The increasing or decreasing of the number of solemnities, maketh not the Testament to come neerer, or depart further from the definition. Indeed the presence or absence of solemnities make the Testament solemne, or unsolemne, but they doe not make it a Testament, or no Testament. . . . Even so an unsolemne Testament doth still remayne a Testament; when these Solemnities doe rather appertaine to the proofe or apparance, then to the substance or Testament. For it is not said in the definition, there must be this or that number of solemnities in the Testament; only it is requisite that there be a just number, that is to say, so many as the law requireth: and if the law require none, the definition requireth none; more then is sufficient for a due proofe. (Swinburne 1611, 21-23 / E4-E6; 1590, 18^{V}–20^{V} / no signature until 21 = E)

Shakespeare's will unquestionably satisfies the requirements of the ordinary Unsolemn Testament of late sixteenth-century English law. However, it also qualifies as a Solemn Testament because it meets the seven requirements of this form as well: (1) a greater number of witnesses than two; (2) the presence of all of them; (3) their personal signatures when possible; (4) the testator's personal signature; (5) no witnesses forbidden to bear testimony; (6) the witnesses seeing the testator and sealing the testament; and (7) the testament's being made at one time.

As I shall demonstrate point by point in the following section, the requisites for the Solemn Testament provide some answers for most of the questions that have arisen over certain aspects of the poet's will. This form also carried within one of its special privileges, namely, the *testamentum inter liberos,* a greater guarantee of validity, which could have been a matter of some concern, owing to certain practices common in his time.

For one thing, litigation over testaments and alleged defamation was rapidly increasing in direct proportion to the declining respect for probate administration. Ralph Houlbrooke's history of this aspect of litigation illustrates this phenomenon using a case from the 1570s in which "it was alleged by Bishop Parkhurst of Norwich and by his successor's chancelor that probate of wills and letters of administration were granted far too quickly. Men were supposedly more willing to suppress or forge wills because they were not required to swear an oath upon them. This neglect of the prescribed safeguards allowed false testaments to be proved and made genuine wills more vulnerable to subsequent attack."[2]

A similar falsifying practice was that of stealing and pirating copies of public material, alluded to by Heminges and Condell in their preface to the *First Folio* as "stolne, and surreptitious copies, maimed, deformed by the frauds and stealthes of injurious impostors" *(First Folio* 7). The evidence seems conclusive that this particular form was the one intended in the devisement.

THE WILL AS A SOLEMN TESTAMENT

> First it is requisite that there be seven witnesses present at the making thereof: Secondly, they must all be required, neither is it sufficient, that they bee present by chaunce, or unrequired: Thirdly, it is required, that every witnesse doo subscribe his name with his owne hand, if he can write, or els two or three others for him. (Swinburne 1611, "a" 19^{V} / $E2^{V}$; 1590, 188^{V} / no signature until 189 = C)

The law reads "seven witnesses." To Shakespeare's will only five names are affixed as witnesses. Of course there would be six if he himself were included, based upon the phrase "In witness whereof I have hereunto put my [seale] *hand.*" A seventh might be managed in the event that Collins's scribe were transcribing the document, as Halliwell-Phillipps suggests, "under the directions of" the supervising lawyer,[3] or if Thomas Russell, named overseer, were also in attendance there. As B. Roland Lewis points out, it was customary for the supervising lawyer to be one of the witnesses, and a third hand does appear in the will, besides that of Shakespeare and that in which it was drawn up (possibly Collins's scribe), in the segment "witnes to the publishing hereof. Fra: Collyns." Moreover, Lewis contends that a *fourth* hand appears to have written in the names of the four witnesses (BRL 2:492 and 473).

But the law was not so procrustean as to require such interpretations, and there is evidence for individual signatures as we shall presently see.

In marginal note *a* to the first requisite, "if anyone be wanting, it is not reputed a solemne testament," one reads, "§ *sed cum paulatim. Instit. de testa. ordin . & ibi Minsing.*" Similarly, with reference to the presence of seven witnesses, marginal note *b* reads, § *sed cum paulatim*" (Swinburne 1611, 19^{V} / $E2^{V}$; 1590, 188^{V} no signature).

The precedent cited in both cases is the *Corpus Juris:*

> Sed cum paulatim tam ex usu hominum quam ex constitutionum emendationibus coepit in unam consonantiam ius civile et praetorium iungi, constitutum est, ut uno eodemque [eo quidem] tempore, quod ius civile quo dammodo exigebat, septem testibus adhibitis et subscriptione testium, quod ex constitutionibus inventum est, et ex edicto praetoris signacula testamentis imponerentur: ut hoc ius tripertitum esse videatur, ut testes quidem et eorum praesentia uno contextu testamenti celebrandi gratia a iure civili descendat, subscriptiones autem testatoris et testium ex sacrarum constitutionum observatione adhibeantur, signacula autem et numerus testium ex edicto 4 praetoris.[4]
>
> [But when, little by little, as human custom brought emendations to the regulations, civil and praetorian law began to be joined into one, it was established at one and the same time, because civil law demanded it in a certain measure and because it was found in the regulations and in the praetorian proclamation, that the seals of the testaments should be placed by seven witnesses who have been summoned, and by the signatures of the witnesses that this law be seen as three-fold, that the witnesses indeed be present in one convening [or gathering] for the sake of solemnizing the testament, as civil law allows, that the signatures of the testator and of the witnesses should be affixed with the care of sacred regulations [ordinances], the seals, on the other hand, and the number of witnesses by praetorian edict should be 4. (My translation.)]

So even the civil law had by custom come to require *four* witnesses present at *one time,* all the names signed and *none excepted.* The next point to be proved, therefore, is that all the names were signed. Claims have been made to the contrary, like those of Lewis, cited previously, and Jane Cox, who holds that "it is not unlikely that Collins' clerk wrote the names" of the witnesses (*Sh/Pub Rec* 34).

Yet the signatures of the four witnesses do not exhibit uniformity. Certain distinctions indicate their having been written in different hands:

the *J*s in *J*ulius Shaw and *J*ohn Robinson do not match, nor do the final *t*s in Hamnet*t* Sadler and Robert Whattcot*t*. Careful examination of the signatures led handwriting analyst Charles Hamilton to conclude that "each is in a very different hand" (*In Search of Shakespeare* 77). And another significant difference between these four signatures and that of Francis Collyns above them is that they appear in the darker ink which clearly differentiates emendations from original text.

The will does meet the first three requisites for a Solemn Testament: the number of witnesses decreed by edict, all required, and each name signed, most probably individually, although the requisites even allow for subscription by another hand, in fact up to "two or three others" in the event a witness cannot write.

There are four remaining requisites to be considered.

SHAKESPEARE'S SIGNATURES

> Fourthly, it is requisite, that the testator doo with his own hande write his name, whom he will shall suceede, and have all his goodes; and if he cannot write, that then he name him before those witnesses. (Swinburne 1611, 19^{V} / E2^{V}; 1590, 188^{V} /no signature)

Shakespeare is generally reckoned to have been very ill by the March 25 date of the redrafting; that he died at New Place; and that it was here, a month before his death, that the solicitor and witnesses were called to make the final draft. Schoenbaum respectfully presents the conclusions of Sir Edward Maunde Thompson (with a word of caution that the terms may be "unwarrantedly diagnostic") regarding "the painful contrast between the handwriting of sickness" in the testamentary signature and "the handwriting of health" in the signature on the deposition. Sir Edward deduced that " 'weakness and malformation of the surname' on the third sheet of the will testify strikingly to 'mortal illness' " (Schoenbaum, *Rec & Images* 99). Schoenbaum agrees that "the indifferent eye may indeed remark the wavering of an unsteady hand in the surname," yet he adopts the view of Halliwell-Phillipps that "it is not necessary to follow the general opinion that the signatures betray the tremulous hand of illness, although portions of them may indicate that they were written from an inconvenient position" (H-P, *Life Abb* 174).

Also pointing toward an inconvenient position from which Shakespeare could write is the fact that the signature most likely to have been the only one newly affixed in March is unique in its position on the page. On the first page only, the one new page, Shakespeare signed in the bottom *left* margin. The fact that it is the most heavily damaged corner may indicate the reason why signatures as a rule were placed in the bottom *right* margin: to avoid being caught in the binding (at the left side) of probate record books. The change in placement may have been due to the dramatist's bedridden condition, in which he was unable to write right-handedly on a far margin. Such a need for an adjustment might also explain the alteration at the end of the will, wherein the words "have hereunto put my seale" were changed to "have hereunto put my *hand.*" The "hand" correction appears in the darker ink and is the only change which appears after that of the second-best bed.

The signatures may of course not be authentic. They may have been "forged" by the clerk, as Cox contends, since not all other wills of the time were signed: "Manuals of the period indicate the form preferred by the doctors of civil law, namely that a will should be signed on every page and witnessed, but virtually any form was acceptable so long as it seemed to be the true representation of the dying man's wishes" (*Sh/ Pub Rec* 34). Yet, as Cox acknowledges, Swinburne was the author of the "leading testamentary manual of the day" (24), and according to Swinburne's treatise, had Shakespeare not signed himself, there would have to have been a stipulation written into the will that he had named the recipient of his goods "before those witnesses."

Since this is not the case, I think it safe to say that the testamentary law provides further evidence supporting the generally accepted view that the Shakespeare signatures are authentic. But at the same time the evidence of the law weakens the claim that the will is a holograph, for if Shakespeare signed the will, then he could not also have written it out, as a comparison of the signatures with the text of the will shows.

REQUISITES FOR WITNESSES

The final three requisites all pertain to witnesses. The fifth requirement enjoins that the witnesses "bee such as are not forbidden to beare testimonie in that behalfe," which, as we observed earlier, they were not. Sixth, "it is necessarie that" they "do see and behold the testator, and not heare him onely" (here again one is referred to a marginal *sed cum paulatim*). They must also "seale the testament, either with their owne seales, or with the seale of another" *(sed cum paulatim).* The seventh and last requisite may be the reason why Collins (or whoever the scrivener was) recopied not the entire document but only the first page and interlineations: "that the testament be made at one time, without any intermission except naturall, such as cannot be avoided" (Swinburne 1611, 19^{V} / E2^{V}; 1590, 188^{V} / CC).

The presence of so many of these requisites—mitigated in each instance by the *sed cum paulatim*—I believe may be taken as a strong indication that Shakespeare wanted a certain kind of document, in fact, the Solemn Testament. The reason for his choice may be inferred from Swinburne's final definition of this kind of document and its attendant guarantees:

> A will thus made is called a solemne testament, which forme if men would observe, (but no man is necessarily tied thereunto heere in England) it were a more safe way, aswell against the forging of false willes, as suppressing of true willes." (Swinburne 1611, 20 / E3; 1590, 189 / CC)

A solemn will was not necessary ("usefull," as Swinburne puts it), but would have assured Shakespeare of a kind of legal guarantee that was not available for his plays. In 1616 the power of the Master of the Revels to license the printing of plays as well as their production had been in effect only nine years. This extension of the Master's function was to ensure some form of protection to playwrights, similar to copyright, of which it was a form, although as Schoenbaum points out, "the word itself does not come into use until the eighteenth century" (*Rec & Images* 205).

The form of the Solemn Testament may also have been selected because it would allow Shakespeare to adopt a further legal device applicable *only* to Solemn Testaments, a device which would provide double protection of his interest from surreptitiousness. This particular device required that the almost total focus of the will be upon his daughters as heirs.

THE CHILDREN AS PRIMARY HEIRS

According to Swinburne, certain types of Solemn Testaments carried "privileges." One such was a testament of the father amongst his children *(testamentum inter liberos):* "that is to say, wherein the father nameth his lawful & naturall children his Executors, giving to them the residue of his goodes, unto which kinde of Testament divers priviledges doe appertaine'' (Swinburne 1611, 32^{V} / $F7^{V}$; 1590, 29 / F). These privileges were (1) if two testaments are found after his death and it cannot be proved which is the valid one, ''that testament is presumed the latter, and so shall prevaile, which is made in favour of the children'' (Swinburne 1611, 32^{V} / $F7^{V}$; 1590, 29 / F); (2) the one in favor of the children ''is not so easily revoked as other testaments are'' (Swinburne 1611, 33 / F8; 1590, 29 / F); and (3) ''the same may take effect, albeit there be no witnesses to proove the same'' (Swinburne 1611, 33^{V} / $F8^{V}$; 1590, 29^{V} / F^{V}). (The last privilege had become subsumed under the Unsolemne Testament by 1611 [23^{V} / $E6^{V}$], and applied to any will ''if it bee written or subscribed with the Testators owne hand or is prooved that the Testator caused the samc to bee written by another'' [33^{V} / $F8^{V}$].)

Such a ''privileged testament'' adds meaning to Shakespeare's lengthy bequest to Susanna and John Hall's children, even unto the eventuality of only a seventh son's survival; thereafter to their daughter Elizabeth or her male issue; or for default of issue, to Judith ''& the heires Males of her bodie lawfullie yssueinge.'' It is undoubtedly just as Schoenbaum says, drawing upon Chambers's view, that in setting up his estate for coming generations Shakespeare had his eye on the future, on the continuation of himself through the male Shakespeares who would come after him (*Sh's Lives* 170–74). B. Roland Lewis, too, sees that in his wanting to establish and continue the Shakespeare family, ''Shakespeare's will is all but unique'' (BRL 2:489).

The choice of testamentary form itself, then, should be seen as a thing of exceptional legal astuteness. By means of the privileged testament, Shakespeare could set forth a legal trust with no loopholes through which false claimants could seize control.

Moreover, in giving Susanna the preponderance of bequests and in naming her and her husband executors, Shakespeare exhibited marked astuteness. The issue was not that Susanna was far and away the favored of the two daughters, even though she might have been. Rather the issue rests in law. A law included by Ranulf de Glanvill, in his great compilation of native law, *Tractatus de legibus et Consuetudinibus Regni Angliae* (1187–1189),[5] and still on the books in Shakespeare's time, that had come down to Shakespeare's day, provides at least one other reason for her father's naming her and John Hall the executors. Unlike the law of primogeniture, wherein house and land normally passed to the eldest son,[6] this law states that if one "leaves several daughters, then the inheritance will clearly be divided between them . . . , but saving the chief messuage to the eldest daughter." Moreover, "husbands of any women whatsoever cannot alienate any part of the inheritance of their wives without the consent of their heirs. . . ." (*Glanvill* 76). This would explain Shakespeare's "legal preoccupations" in the will with "transference through the female line," as Knight puts it (270).

The Glanvill law may further provide us with a clue as to Shakespeare's choice of the word "neece" (or what has been read as this) in referring to his granddaughter Elizabeth Hall. Of course, as Schoenbaum points out, " 'niece' at this time could still carry the now obsolete sense of 'granddaughter,' a usage found (Halliwell-Phillipps observes) in the Wycliffite Bible" (*Comp Doc Life* 299). But the word could have been adopted for its approximation to the legal term Glanvill used in legal documents for granddaughters, "neptis(es)" (bk. 7, 77), the Latin derivation for *niece*.

The Glanvill law prescribing the naming of daughters, that is, the transference through the female line, furnishes a legal explanation for the deletion of "sonne in L" from the new first page rather than the subjective one commonly given—that he disliked his son-in-law Quiney. Of course this is not to say that he may not have liked his son-in-law. There is, however, more basis for believing he disliked Quiney, considering his new son-in-law's disgraceful trial, than for accepting the suppositions made by Charles Hamilton that he "despised" his daughter Judith (*In Search of Shakespeare: A Reconnaissance into the Poet's Life and Handwriting* 249) and had wished that she instead of her twin brother Hamnet had died (91), or that Judith and Quiney conspired in a murder plot against her father (88–105).

On the other hand, it may well have been confidence in Susanna's husband John Hall that decided who was named executor. For being executor or administrator carried many responsibilities. According to Blackstone, the executor "is bound to perform a will [take it to probate]; . . . . he is chargeable with the debts of the deceased, so far as assets come to his hands: and, as against creditors in general, shall be allowed all payments made to any other creditor in the same or a superior degree, himself [507] only excepted. . . . He must bury the deceased; he must prove the will of the deceased. . . . [and he] is to make an inventory of all the goods and chattels and. . . . to collect all the goods and chattels so inventoried [510] . . . and pay the debts of the deceased" (510–11).

Judith had first place even in the original draft as the three lines remaining of that version at the top of page 2 indicate. When the new first sheet was made after her marriage, only the part pertaining to her needed to be recast. Her position could reflect a father's placing the child first for whom he felt the most protective concern: compare the marked through phrase in the original draft at the top of page 2, "for her best proffitt vntil her Mariage," to the notation written into the new first sheet, "for the best benefitt of her & her issue." The other daughter, Susanna, had been married for nine years when the will was drawn up. That he had such a distinction at the forefront of his mind may be further demonstrated by a detail George Russell French noticed, "that he refers to Susanna as 'my daughter Susanna Hall,' but to her sister as 'my daughter Judith,' no fewer than five times, and does not allude to her marrying except in prospect" (*Shaksp Geneal* 381).

Shakespeare's primary concern seems to have been for Judith's security. She was thirty-one years old when she married Quiney, who was four years her junior. In stipulating that Judith's husband must settle on her an estate in kind equivalent in value to the bequest of £150, a sum considerable for that time, Shakespeare seems to have been forcing Thomas Quiney to acknowledge both the office and the duties of *husband*. Moreover, the family settlement in which Judith had to release rights to the Copiehold further underscores a move to force Quiney to provide a home for his wife and not to become a holder of any of Shakespeare's holdings. We know that Judith complied with the terms of the settlement from a record of 1617 noting a payment of 2 shillings and six pence by "John Haule gen. and Susan his wief for the Fyne of admyttance of the said Susan unto one cottage in Stratford after the decease of Wm. Shakespere, gen. late father of the said Susan" (Bentley 43), presumably the cottage cited in the will.

Judith's new state as a married woman may also have brought about the change in the bequest of the poet's plate: to his granddaughter instead of to her. As a married woman, she might expect her husband to provide either plate or the means for purchasing their own plate. However, Judith is given special mention a second time as well, toward the end. It appears in both the first and final drafts: "I gyve & bequeath to my saied daughter Judith my broad silver gilt bole." This very personal and particular bequest—presumably something he held in esteem or something that had special meaning to the two of them—seems a touching gesture toward his younger daughter, as Halliwell-Phillipps attests, "an unmistakable testimony of affection" (H-P, *Life Abb* 176). Judith's subsequent long life further points to devotion for her father and faithfulness to her marriage. She had three sons, all of whom were baptized in the parish church at Stratford: the first named for her father, Shakespeare Quiney, and the following two for the two Quiney family members who had been Shakespeare's friends, Richard and Thomas. She outlived all three of her sons, who died at the ages of six months, twenty-one years, and nineteen years, respectively (Bentley 33), and her husband. She herself died in 1662 and is also buried at Stratford.

In light of the special concern reflected in the altered first page along with the special bequest and Judith's subsequent years, the privileged testament seems a likely explanation for the division of property. The privileged testament would also account for the exclusion of his wife, except for the one bequest specified for her. The stipulations therein do away with the myths that have grown around the small inheritance bequeathed to Anne Shakespeare. Schoenbaum has a good summation of the main lines of the debate over what was to "arouse fierce contention": "Does the meagerness of the bequest betray indifference or derision? Or had this object sentimental associations that did not attach to the best bed, which was perhaps reserved for overnight guests at New Place?" (*Sh's Lives* 46).

In point of fact, under the terms of the *privileged testament* Anne Shakespeare would not be cited. In such a devisement she had to be excluded as a major beneficiary to protect her own interests as well as those of the children. Further, the legal reality was that no bequest was necessary, for Anne was entitled to a third of the estate anyway.

As may be inferred from one of the law books current in Shakespeare's day, John Rastell's *An Exposition of Certaine Difficult and Obscure Words, and Termes of the Lawes of this Realme. . . . unto are also added the Old Tenures:* the wife was to receive "the third part of all that there was to her husband in his life, in fee simple or fee taile, and she shall holde these landes for terme of her life as her free holde."[7] As Schoenbaum points out in his study of Shakespeare's biographers, *Shakespeare's Lives,* it was Charles Knight who first "grounded an explanation in the law itself" (387). Knight consulted lawyers on his discovery that since all of Shakespeare's properties with the exception of the copyhold tenement were freehold, his wife was entitled to dower. " 'She was provided for amply, by the clear and undeniable operation of the English law' " (qtd. in *Sh's Lives* 386). Schoenbaum concludes that "English common law entitled Anne to a life interest of one third in her husband's estate, as well as to residence in the family house. That was her dower right" (*Doc Life* 247).

Ironically, one argument in the camp of those who hold that Shakespeare deliberately intended to neglect Anne is also based upon the proposition that common law entered into Shakespeare's arrangements, the very dower law that I am proposing as in fact protecting her interests. For example, Sir Sidney Lee contended that Anne was denied "a dower right in the estate, for English common law barred a widow's claim on property of which her husband did not hold sole proprietorship" [such as the Blackfriars Gatehouse]. Therefore Lee argues that Shakespeare "had the intention of excluding her from the enjoyment of his possessions after death."[8] Yet as Schoenbaum points out, "Shakespeare did not establish conditions that would negate his widow's interest in his other possessions, some of which were more valuable than the Blackfriars Lodging" (*Rec & Images* 43).

What this means is that exclusion of reference to Anne was deliberate because it was essential for the fulfillment of not one but two points of law, namely (1) that of the *privileged testament* with its guarantee of sole validity, and (2) that of dower rights. The guarantees of the privileged testament were assured by the incontestability of the Solemn Testament still recognized by doctors of civil law in Shakespeare's day though, as we have seen, being supplanted by the general adoption of the unsolemn testamentary form. Dower rights too had come to that time from ancient observance and from another branch of law long observed in England, the common law. As Jane Cox found from examining over 150 wills that were proved the same year as Shakespeare's, "The concept of a wife's entitlement to one third of her husband's real estate for life and one third of his personal estate was still very much alive" (*Sh/Pub Rec* 127).

Like the Solemn Testament, dower rights too passed from general observance during this period of legal history. The law governing dower rights is therefore another area of law the reader may find unfamiliar. The following brief history of this law will establish the validity of Anne's dower rights and thereby conclude my resolution of the major controversies in the light of testamentary law. At the same time I will be setting the stage for the subject of the next chapter, the second best bed and the remaining force of ecclesiastical law.

DOWER RIGHTS

Dower rights refer to the life interest of the widow in a third part of her husband's lands, the other two parts being his and their children's. The exact origins of the law of dower and the wife's property inheritance are unknown, but the ancient Anglo-Saxon law codes offer an interesting precedent. Dorothy Whitelock traces bequest of property to "the thegn Thurstan" who gave property in Norfolk to his wife *to mund and to maldage,"* a phrase which occurs in Scandinavian law codes and for which Whitelock gives the translation: "as I gave it to her before as a marriage payment and in accordance with our contract."[9]

The third portion to the wife, the thing that is pertinent to Shakespeare's will, goes back at least as far as the seventh-century laws of King Ine of Wessex (688–726 A.D.), although the practice must have begun earlier, for in Ine it is mentioned as a thing known or so familiar that there was no need to define it. Here it is enacted that even if the husband steals cattle and brings it into his house, if the wife declares by oath that she didn't eat any, "she is to receive her third portion" (*Eng Hist Doc* 406).

In the twelfth-century Glanvill covers dower and the wife's rights in relation to it in the *Tractatus*. His use of the word "dos" for "dower" was the common practice among English writers (*Commentaries* II, ch. 8, 129):

> The word "dos" has two meanings. In common English law usage it means that which a freeman gives to his wife at the church door at the time of his marriage. For every man is bound both by ecclesiastical and by secular law to endow his wife at the time of his marriage. When a man endows his wife at the time of his marriage. When a man endows his wife either he nominates certain property as dower, or he does not. If he does not nominate dower, then one third of the whole of his free tenement is deemed to be her dower, and the reasonable dower of any woman is one third of the whole of the free tenement of which her husband was seised in demesne at the time of the marriage. If, however, the husband nominates dower and it amounts to more than one third, it cannot stand at such a level, but will be measured up to one third; for a man can give less but not more than one third of his tenement in dower. . . . Legally a woman is completely in the power of her husband. (*Glanvill*, bk. 6, 58 ff.)

That dower continued to be upheld into the next century, following Glanvill, is evident from the work of the great thirteenth-century legal historian Judge Bracton, who, Professor Heinrich Brunner claimed, "gives the fullest account of English law of the Middle Ages" (*SEAALH* 2:35). Bracton specified the provision as well as the place of provision for dower:

> Dower is that which a free man gives his spouse at the church door [on the marriage day], because of the burden of matrimony and the future marriage, for the maintenance of the wife and the nurture of the children when they are born, should the husband predecease her. . . . the rightful dower of every woman is the third part of all the lands and tenements her husband held in his demesne and so in fee that he could endow her on the day he married her. . . . When dower is become law, a wife is sufficiently endowed though her husband say nothing.[10]

According to Sir William S. Holdsworth (*Hist Eng Law* 3:523) a wife from "early days had a right to a third of the chattels if she survived her husband, of which right probably the husband could not deprive her by his will." In the days of both Glanvill and Bracton "a man['s] . . . wife and children had certain rights to his property, of which he could not deprive them by his will" (550). The only part which a man was free to dispose of as he pleased was that which remained over and above the two-thirds going to his wife and those children who had not received an advancement from their father in his lifetime. Moreover, this custom was so widespread in the twelfth and thirteenth centuries that "the common law knew a special writ, called the writ *de rationabili parte bonorum,* by means of which the wife and children could get their shares." This scheme of succession, "once part of the general law of England," was "devised before the ecclesiastical jurisdiction on matters testamentary had been consolidated" (550–51).

Continuance of dower rights is further confirmed by the *Commentaries on the Laws of England,*[11] where Sir William Blackstone defines the laws involved in the disposition of a man's goods as *jura rerum,* "rights of things," in other words, property law. This law in turn was subdivided into "the law of immoveables as opposed to moveables, or land as opposed to chattels" (*Commentaries* iii and v). To Blackstone, "the reason, which our law gives for adopting it [dower rights], is a very plain and sensible one; for the sustenance of the wife, and the nurture and education of the younger children" (II, ch. 8, 131). "A widow may be endowed of all her husband's lands, tenements, and hereditaments, corporeal or incorporeal, under the restrictions before-mentioned; unless there be some special reason to the contrary" (II, ch. 8, 132).

In fact, it was the large number of specific legacies of movables that became, in Holdsworth's words, "the most striking characteristic of the medieval will." The contents of a testator's whole house "can often be pictured with fair accuracy from the various legacies in his will'' (*Hist Eng Law* 3:546). This is evident from Furnivall's collection of fifty wills in *Wills and Inventories,* where the specific legacy first appears in 1400 and where it is still being applied in 1522.

An act of Parliament on April 23 in the thirty-first year of King Henry's VIII's reign, to be dated as of May 1, 1536, legislated the dower law, which, as Swinburne makes indisputably clear, was upheld and recognized throughout the land in Shakespeare's day. In the case, for instance, where there was ''no 'jointer' upon the wife's claim, then she shall be admitted and inabled to pursue, have and demand her dower, by write *[sic]* of dower, after the due course and order of the common lawes of this realme: this act or any law or provision made to the contrarie thereof not withstanding'' (Swinburne 1590, L7^{V}).

In the *Calendar of Wills, proved and enrolled in the Court of Husting, London, A.D. 1258–1688,*[12] the will of one Richard Lewen, a brewer, in the year 1568 further establishes the conventionality of dower:

> His goods and chattels to be divided into three equal parts, *according to the laudable custom* [my italics], one of which he leaves to Johan his wife, another to John and William his sons, [& daughters] [bracketed material is as it appears in the original] and the third part he reserves to himself.

Of course one doesn't know with certainty about Stratford, as E. K. Chambers early acknowledged:

> If no equivalent jointure had been substituted, as to which there is no evidence, Mrs. Shakespeare would have been entitled by common law to her dower of a life interest in one-third of any of the testator's heritable estates on which dower had not, as in the case of the Blackfriars property, been legally barred; and to residence in his principal mansion house. . . . Whether or not the widow was entitled to a third of personalty . . . depended upon local custom; the Warwickshire custom is unknown. Such legal or customary rights are sometimes incorporated in the provisions of wills, sometimes not; they would be operative in any event. (EKC 2:176–77)

Such reluctance to generalize about legal practice was shared by E. Vine Hall in *Testamentary Papers II: Wills from Shakespeare's Town and Time,* where he echoes Chambers, saying that the widow's share ''depended upon local custom; the Warwickshire custom is unknown.''[13]

Citing Sir Edward Coke's opinion, "that the law [of property] had changed so much that a testator was in the early seventeenth century enabled to divest his widow and children of all his personal property, by making testamentary bequest to others, except that the widow might not be deprived of her paraphernalia," Green finds support in Swinburne's *Treatise:*

> And in the opinion of some, the Law of this land, which leaveth all the residue to the dispoſition of the Testator . . . seemeth to haue better ground in reaſon, then the custome, whereby he is forced eyther to leue two parts of three, or at least the one half to his wife and children. For what if the ſonne be an vnthrift, or naughty perſon? What if the wife be not onely a sharpe shrew, but perhaps of worse conditions? (275–76)

The custom of dower is, as Schoenbaum has drawn to our attention, "more complicated than at first appears. A widow's portion comprised both land and chattels. With respect to land, custom appears to have operated fairly uniformly, the widow's right being recognized from early until modern times. . . . As regards chattels, custom varied from borough to borough. One would like to know more about Stratford practice. Wills do not provide the answer, for *custom functions when the wills are silent*" (*Comp Doc Life* 301). I have emphasized the last sentence, for in it, I believe, is the key to our understanding of some of the assumptions upon which the bequests in the will were based.

It is possible that in Shakespeare's case the will is "silent" because the custom of the dower law was still functioning. To this may be added the further weight carried by the Solemn Testament. True, as a testamentary form it was no longer required in English law, yet all the points Swinburne cites as requisite to it are present in Shakespeare's will—*sed cum paulatim.*

Or to put it another way, we could say that all the major "questions" regarding the will—that is, the number and presence of witnesses, the signatures of witnesses and testator, the different hands noted, the character of the witnesses, the alteration of only one full page with interlineations allowed to stand, and the preponderance of bequests to the children to the exclusion of the wife—all these find an explanation in the Solemn Testamentary form. The privileged testament of *testamentum inter liberos* included within the Solemn Testament carried the legal weight of double protection of validity. As a legal document, Shakespeare's will could certainly withstand any upheaval within the structure of English law such as that underway at the very time in which the will was written.

The dower law, "subject to difference of local custom," has been traced by Melville Madison Bigelow up to the reign of Charles II, by which time personalty, that is, personal property or chattels, might be disposed of by will freely in the greater part of England. According to Bigelow, the claims of the widow continued in force after those of the children had disappeared (*SEAALH* 3:780). Holdsworth finds evidence that the wife's dower rights continued up to 1685, indeed that the restraints upon testation imposed by this scheme appear to have been observed till 1692 in the province of York, till 1724 in London, and even in certain divergent cases as late as 1856 (*Hist Eng Law* 3:561). The significant point is that it was in Shakespeare's own time that the alteration of such conditions began.

In the transformation that occurred within the English legal system during the 16th and 17th centuries, the Solemn Testament, like the dower law, was simply supplanted, becoming buried from view. The upheaval likewise accounts for the obscuring of those laws that directly pertain to the term "second best" in the notorious bequest of the poet's will.

Blackstone lamented the changing tide of law which he saw reflected in the history of this very dower law, this law which "stood in the reign of Henry the Second" and "continued to be the law of the land at the time of *magna carta*":

> In the reign of King Edward the Third this right of the wife and children was still held to be the universal or common law. . . . and Sir Henry Finch lays it down expressly, in the reign of Charles the First, to be the general law of the land. But this law is at present altered by imperceptible degrees, and the deceased may now by will bequeath the whole of his goods and chattels; though we cannot trace out when first this alteration began.

Blackstone saw in the passing of the rights of the "lord and the church" the demise of the protective dower rights of the wife. And his statement brings forward the two old common laws from which originated the fixed phrase "second best":

> Thus is the old common law now utterly abolished throughout all the Kingdom of England. . . . In disposing of which [all his chattels] he was bound by the custom of many places . . . to remember his lord and the

> church, by leaving them his two best chattels, of which was the original of heriots and mortuaries; and afterward he was left at his own liberty, to bequeath the remainder as he pleased. (*Commentaries* 2:492–93)

It was in tracing the history of these medieval institutions of *heriots* and *mortuaries* which Blackstone laments in the above passage as being lost forever, that I unearthed a new meaning for the term "second best." But this controversial allusion in Shakespeare's will pertains to another kind of legal tradition, the ecclesiastical or canon law, and I believe ramifications of the bequest will become more evident to the reader if presented within the context of the legal changes that buried these institutions, along with the Solemn Testament form, from view.

In various legal components of Shakespeare's will may be seen the residue of the shifting systems within English law itself. As we have seen in this chapter all points of the will are upheld by common, or civil, law. Moreover, through its inviolable application of classical testamentary common law in its English adaptation—the Solemn Testament—the will provided unconditionally guaranteed protection against spurious claims.

Yet the singular bequest to his wife, as I will show in Chapter Four, reflects both its old ecclesiastical origin and what of its intention had passed into custom. In addition, it drew upon the old ecclesiastical-based common laws, such as the chief messuage to the eldest daughter and dower rights, yet at the same time clearly reflected the new shifts toward legal refinement in strategies that would have proven unassailable even in civil courts of law.

Furthermore, it contains a choice example of the way in which an old ecclesiastical law survived as custom. The same kind of "mix" we find in the will becomes evident as we begin our search for the roots of the three branches of English law that led up to the situation such as existed in Renaissance England. If we turn to the times in which the will was devised, and trace these three branches to their roots, we can get a sharp focus on the significance of the shifts taking place in the legal system of Shakespeare's day and how these shifts generated a marked revival of interest in the old laws.

We find, for example, that the old laws, indeed the sourcebooks I have used in my study, were kept very much before the public eye in Renaissance England, most notably in the continuance of power vested in ecclesiastical courts and in the emergence of two public movements, the one that has come to be known as the Elizabethan Gothic Revival and that related to the activities of Recusants. We also find abundant evidence to support the claim that both the old civil and canon laws and customs were an intentional consideration in the making of the will, and further, that Shakespeare had personal knowledge of them. The strong evidence that both Shakespeare and his family had personal ties with these and other areas of life in which the old laws were kept alive is the conclusive proof I offer for the claims made in my study that the will must be read in the context of medieval and Renaissance legal backgrounds.

Chapter Three

The Will and the Times

Time: it is in my pow'r
To o'erthrow law, and in one self-born hour
To plant and o'erwhelm custom. . . . I witness to
The times that brought them in.

The Winter's Tale, IV.i.7–11

We have seen how Shakespeare's will may be viewed as "witness to the times" that brought it in with regard to its retention of the Old Solemn Testamentary form at a time when the new unsolemn form had supplanted it. In this chapter I shall attempt to show that change against the background, or larger context, of changes taking place at the very base of English law itself, and this will introduce us to another area of law to which the will further bears "witness to the times," in its second best bequest.

Time's monologue serves well as text for this chapter, for in the juxtaposition of law and custom and the disparate actions wrought upon them—"o'erthrow," "plant," and "o'erwhelm"—all within the space of but two lines, may be seen something of the dynamics of upheaval at work in English law during Shakespeare's lifetime. Such dynamics of displacement were set in motion not only in regard to individual laws, but extended to the very foundations of English law, that is, the ancient branches of civil, ecclesiastical (or canon), and common law. These centuries-old foundations of the English legal system were "o'erthrown," new customs "planted" and "o'erwhelmed," within the comparatively brief "self-born hour" of a few decades.

Yet, dramatic and profoundly rending as the initiating actions were, the changes themselves were often long in becoming established, creating the kind of situation seen in the preceding chapter with regard to civil testamentary forms, where the old and the new might be found overlapping for a period of years. Even while the Solemn Testament was being supplanted or ''o'erthrown'' by the Unsolemn Testament, the old form as legal model was still recognized as viable, *sed cum paulatim.* Shakespeare's will was legal in either case, upheld by the old Solemn Testamentary law and in all other respects meeting the requirements of the new unsolemn form.

Similarly, the civil and ecclesiastical jurisdictions began to overlap. What had been strictly of concern to the ecclesiastical courts—for example, jurisdiction in tithe and testament matters—might now be brought before the courts of common law as well. The overlay made for a complex interdependence, but it also made for confusion, increased litigation, and rising interest in things legal. The common perception of the consequences may have been given expression in what W. H. Elton identifies as ''a favourite metaphor'' of the age—the '' 'world upside down'.''[1]

That it was an age of constitutional reform was evident. The ancient civil and ecclesiastical (or canon) systems were being subsumed by common law. All educated people would have been aware of it, those in the legal professions, as one might expect, particularly so. In his study of the period, *Church Courts, Sex and Marriage in England, 1570–1640,* Martin Ingram characterizes it as a time of ''assimilation,'' during which ''ecclesiastical jurists were working to assimilate the old and new elements in church law.''[2] In fact, Ingram cites as one of the ''major works of ecclesiastical jurisprudence'' the source I use as basis for my argument in Chapter Two, Swinburne's *A Briefe Treatise of Testaments and Last Willes.*

In the Preface to this work Henry Swinburne makes direct reference to this state of affairs as the primary reason for having undertaken the compilation of testamentary laws, an effort from which scholars today gain immeasurably, though to the professional legalists of his own time he felt obliged to apologize for seeming ''to bring water to the sea or owls to Athens'' in presenting a compilation of testamentary laws. His work is of particularly great value as a source which uniquely presents English law in its most crucial stage of development, when ecclesiastical law was being subsumed by civil or common law, a merging which, by an ironic turn, resulted from the severance of civil from canon law by ''Henrie the eighth of famous and happie memorie'' in 25 Hen. 8, ch. 19:

> It was enacted and established (amongst other Statutes then made, and since that time revived in the first yeere of her Maiesties most gracious

> reigne that nowe is) that such lawes ecclesiasticall being then already made, which bee not hurtfull or prejudiciall to the prerogative roiall, nor repugnant to the lawes, statutes, and customes of this Realme, shall still be used and executed as they were before the making of that act. . . . Which lawes so established, revived and confirmed . . . are termed . . . *the Kings Ecclesiasticall Lawes.*
>
> Whereas also the Civill Law ever since the Ecclesiasticall Law was made, had beene deemed and judged for part and parcell of the same Ecclesiasticall Law, in cases wherein it doth not differ from the same. For whereas these two lawes be not contrarie, the one is suppletorie of the other, and being mutually incorporated doe both make one bodie; otherwise the Civill Law being contradicted by the Ecclesiasticall law, ought to be silent in the Ecclesiasticall court. (1611, pp. ii–iii / sigs. A7, A7^{V}–A8; 1590, ii–iii / B10 *[sic]* –B10^{V} and B2)

Swinburne "thought it not only not superfluous, but expedient . . . to make collection of the most principall Lawes, Civill and Ecclesiasticall, pertayning to Testaments":

> [The laws were] scattered and dispersed here and there, and secretly hidden from the subjects of this realme in corners of many bookes of strange Countries, and forreine Language, intangled also and incombred with long discourses of farre different argument, and no lesse number of lawes utterly impertinent to the government of this commonwealth. (1611, A8^{V}; 1590, iv / B2)

Without Swinburne's discernment of the magnitude of change during his time and his dedicated interest in collecting and preserving these laws, neither the lawyers of his day nor readers of Chapter Two of my study would have had a sourcebook so readily available for searching precedence without incurring a great deal of expense.

In this chapter I will draw upon another sourcebook resulting from a similar impetus in Shakespeare's day toward the collection and preservation of ancient laws, William Lambarde's *Archaionomia.* In the caring efforts of the Antiquarians like Lambarde and others among Shakespeare's contemporaries we shall find laws that provide a new explanation of the second best bequest as well as the evidence for Shakespeare's probable personal knowledge of these laws—and not only Shakespeare's personal knowledge, but his family's, too.

If we look to Time's monologue again, we have to think that if the allusion is an indication of Shakespeare's awareness of the changing dynamics of the age, it also illustrates another point, one that must be kept in mind in considering "new" explanations of the second best. Surely the fact that there are so many legal allusions in the plays shows that Shakespeare drew upon the currency of the public's fascination with law courts during this period: "people found attending the courts and watching judicial procedure a dramatic and diverting pastime" (Phillips 35). For certainly Shakespeare expected his audience to understand the allusions. I think a similar claim should be made regarding the so-called "problematical" points in Shakespeare's will. Because of the long-standing usage of these points in ancient civil and ecclesiastical law and custom, they would surely have been understood by—or at the least would have been familiar to—both those remembered in the will and those responsible for its execution and probate. It is because of the long-standing discontinuance that they can be misunderstood by the reader today.

I hope to remedy the situation for the reader by recalling here some of the historical background of English law prior to the upheaval in order to identify the major changes and movements that ensued during the time in which the will was devised. By thus temporarily diverting the reader's attention from the will itself, I hope to take the reader into the shoes of Time, stepping into or witnessing the times, as it were, of the will's devisement, so that thereafter, returning to the will, it may be read in a new light.

HISTORICAL BACKGROUND

As late as 1580 three kinds of law were still being recognized. In his *Description of England* (1580),[3] William Harrison explained them. The first is " 'ciuill, vsed in the chancerie, Admiraltie, and diuerse other courts'; [second] . . . canon law, 'dailie practised among vs, especiallie in cases of tithes, contracts of matrimonie, and such like, as are vsuallie to be seene in the consistories of our bishops (and higher courts of the two archbishops) where the exercise of the same is verie hotlie followed' and the third sort 'are our owne, consisting of Statute law, which is made by Parliament, Common law, which standeth vpon sundrie maximes or principles and yeares or termes, which doo conteine such cases as by great studie and solemn argument of the iudges . . . and thereto the deepest reach and foundations of reason, are ruled and adiudged for law, and Customarie law' " (qtd. in Johansson, n. 11, 8).

By tracing these three branches to their roots, we can get a sharp focus on the significance of the shifts taking place in the legal system of Shakespeare's day and how these shifts generated a marked revival of interest in the old laws.

A momentous displacement was occurring in the history of English law. Indeed, in its balance of various legal components, Shakespeare's will may be seen as very much a product of the shifting systems within English law itself, poised at the watershed of its own history. All points of the will are upheld by common, or civil, law, as we have seen, yet the singular bequest to his wife, as I will demonstrate in Chapter Four, reflects both its old ecclesiastical origin and what of its intention had passed into custom. Moreover, through its inviolable application of classical testamentary common law in its English adaptation—the Solemn Testament—the will provided unconditionally guaranteed protection against spurious claims. In addition, it drew upon the old ecclesiastical-based common laws, such as the chief messuage to the eldest daughter and dower rights, yet at the same time clearly reflected the new shifts toward legal refinement in strategies that would have proven unassailable even in civil courts of law.

Furthermore, the will contains a choice example of the way in which an old ecclesiastical law survived as custom. The same kind of "mix" we find in the will becomes evident as we begin our search for the roots of the three branches of English law that led up to the situation such as existed in Renaissance England.

Early English law, like all early civil law, was rooted in tribal custom; however, as a result of the conversion of the Anglo-Saxons to Christianity, it became densely interwoven with ecclesiastical precepts. The oldest statutes or laws *(dómas, gerædnessa, ásetnysse)* of the *witenagemot* were a combination of new ecclesiastically influenced law and codification of existing customary laws. But the question is not simple—as even a brief survey like the following will indicate—because ecclesiastical law, like Saxon England, was itself mixed up with Roman law. As Dorothy Whitelock points out in the Preface to *Councils and Synods,* "It is rarely possible to draw a line between an ecclesiastical synod and a meeting of the witan" (vi), although after 1066 it was clearer that clergy and bishops' councils were formed (ix).

According to Maitland, already by about A.D. 350 a pagan sacrifice was by the letter of the law a capital crime (*SEAALH,* 1:10). In c. 380 (Maitland places it tentatively at 385 in the decretal of Pope Siricius, 11), Theodosius claimed the bishop of Rome as legislator so that bishops gained disciplinary jurisdiction over clergy and laity. Two statute books appeared in the fifth century, that of Theodosius, a Spanish general, in 438 and that of Euric the West Goth between 470 and 475, in which Germanic law was collected. Maitland refers to a kinship between Spanish and Icelandic law of the time and between Saxon England and Lombard Italy, a kinship reflected in the preservation of archaic forms in the Scandinavian law when it was written in the thirteenth century. By the sixth century books of ecclesiastical law were being compiled (SEAALH, 1:13). In c. 500 Dionysius Exiguus collected and translated the canons of Eastern councils and decretal letters into the *Corpus Juris Canonici* and *Collectio Dionysiana,* the latter of which may have been present and used by Archbishop Theodore in 673 at the Council of Hertford (SEAALH, 1:16).

William K. Boyd sees Constantine's introduction of the episcopal court into the judicial system as a turning point: "episcopal arbitration was transformed into a legal mode of procedure."[4] The clergy now began to have influence in public life. Boyd traces direct transmission of Roman imperial law through, primarily, the *Lex Romana Visigothorum* or *Breviary of Alaric* (approved in 506 by a council of bishops and nobles "with the command that in the future no other source of law should be used by Roman subjects") (110), and secondarily, the code and *Novels* of Justinian in the sixth and seventh centuries, combined with later development of Visigothic law in Spain. Testamentary law was greatly affected by the activity of the episcopacy in the administration of justice. (For Justinian's influence, see Boyd, n. 62.)

From the ninth century to the close of the Middle Ages Canon Law was recognized as binding and strongly influenced all levels of life. Edgar's and Canute's ecclesiastical laws are illustrations. The ecclesiastical courts (or Courts of the Ordinary, as they were also called, because the archdeacon could be an ordinary priest given judicial power by a bishop) had jurisdiction affecting the subjects of the realm in three matters: (1) pecuniary, such as tithes; (2) matrimonial causes, such as the validity of marriage, legitimacy, divorce, etc.; and (3) testamentary causes and the administration of the estates of intestates. In the next stage of development, however, at the Norman Conquest the law of England was converted into a *lex terrae,* a true local law, and William the Conqueror set up a system of separate courts for secular and ecclesiastical business. The King's Court dominated the development of law. Latin superseded Anglo-Saxon as the language of law, alternating with French. In 1070–76 the *Episcopales Leges* was introduced, a statute concerning separation of ecclesiastical from secular jurisdictions. With the appearance of the great Domesday Book toward the end of William I's reign, men began to speak of the common law.

Then by mid-twelfth century a civil law revival strengthened the position of the secular system. Glanvill's definition of common law leaves no doubt as to the authority which it had attained: "the settled law of the king's court, common to all free men in the sense that it is available to them in civil causes if they will have it, and applicable against them in serious criminal causes whether they like it or not" (*Glanvill* xi).

By the close of the thirteenth century the English Parliament was established and law had become the command of the state, the law of the Royal Court. Statute law was established with the reign of Henry III, the first Year Book produced in 1292. The *jus commune* of the Western church was administered in the ecclesiastical courts, the common law in the royal courts. Bracton was a representative figure of the times: as a clergyman he would have known something of canon law since he served as cathedral chancellor, and yet he also knew the law of the bench as an experienced royal justice under Henry III (Jenks, *SEAALH* 1:165). The legal system, cultivated from its beginning by the church and reflecting the values with which it had been inculcated, had thus attained a stature and measure of power of its own.

The letters LL.B. stand for Bachelor of Both Laws, the laws referred to being the canon and the civil law.[5] In fact, one of the influences of canon law upon common law was the jurisdiction of church courts over the administration of estates of movables of persons deceased (Keeton 58). The Inns of Court became, in the words of Coke, "the most famous University for the profession of law only, or of any one human science in the world," where students were educated in Common Law (89–90). In this connection, the reader may recall the site where Shakespeare's will was first on public display—Doctors' Commons, which belonged to a society of lawyers in London forming a distinct profession for the practice of the civil and canon laws (see Chapter One).

An English common lawyer might not have knowledge of sacramental theology from canon law, though he would have known of the ecclesiastical law of wills, either from having inherited himself or probably from having served as executor.

However, in the sixteenth century the relations between church and state began to break down. Roman civil law was beginning to exercise strong influence, even though the law was decidedly English. From the time of Henry VII (1485–1509) the language of legislation was English exclusively. Following Henry VIII's divorce from Catherine of Aragon, relations between the courts were irrevocably altered. In 1535 Henry forbade the study of canon law and encouraged the study of civil law by the foundation of professorships at Oxford in 1535 and Cambridge in 1540.[6] The crown became supreme over all persons and causes. The canon law of the Western church was to give place to the "King's Ecclesiastical Law of the Church of England." The clergy also recognized the royal supremacy so far as the law of Christ allows. The organization of ecclesiastical courts was maintained, but the king had put himself in the place of the pope. The King's ecclesiastical law administered by civilians was put in place of the canon law of Rome. The ecclesiastical law of England became national, like the church itself. The church was brought within the state. And law, like society in the late medieval world, became secularized.[7]

Thus, in a really anomalous twist, ecclesiastical law, which had originally been such a powerful shaping influence in bringing forth a common law from tribal custom, found itself assimilated by that very law, then separated from it, and ultimately supplanted by it, surviving for the most part as mere custom.

ECCLESIASTICAL COURTS IN SHAKESPEARE'S TIME

By Shakespeare's day, although ecclesiastical authority had been weakened compared with that of the civil courts, the church still had recourse to its law through the ecclesiastical courts, anciently called, according to Coke, *Halimots* (i.e. Holy Courts), *Circgemots,* or *Chircgemots* (pt. 4, 321). Everyone in the land was subject to both the royal and the canonical systems. The division was one with which the people had long had to live. As Mark Edwin Andrews thoroughly explains in *Law versus Equity in "The Merchant of Venice,"* there had long been a "conflict between the common law courts which dispersed unmitigated 'justice' by the strict letter of the law, and the courts of Chancery where 'mercy seasons justice,' to do equity." Since 1300 English common law had been "rigid and restricted," while equity was "flexible and free." From 1330, when King Edward III "decided to allow his Chancellor to hear cases which judges would not hear," with the intent of thereby increasing his own revenue while also aiding his subjects, the people had recourse to either of the two systems. "The common law courts acted *in rem* on the property of the litigants; the equity courts acted *in personam* on the person of the litigants'' (xi). This conflict lasted approximately three hundred years, until Coke's case in 1615 (Glanvill vs. Courtney). (Andrews believes *The Merchant of Venice* dramatizes both the problem and the victory of this case.) Of all the kinds of courts surveyed by Andrews, only the ecclesiastical ones were excluded. Hence it is no surprise to find that as early as 1245 there was need for a little manual of procedure brought out by one Mr. Richardson.[8]

As R. H. Helmholz explains in *Roman Canon Law in Reformation England,* ''Knowledge of Roman law in the sixteenth century led naturally, almost inevitably, to knowedge of the canon law. . . . The interdependence of the two laws certainly obtained in any serious study of English ecclesiastical law'' (151). The two systems actually represented the two foundations of English law: civil and canon law. From canon law stemmed the system based upon equity, or mercy; from civil law, the system upholding the letter of the law.

ECCLESIASTICAL COURT OF STRATFORD

Ecclesiastical law was probably held in respect in Stratford, and certain laws and practices are relevant to Shakespeare's will as I will bring forward in the discussion of its religious implications in the following chapter. For example, the organization of the Gild of Holy Cross, from its beginning in the thirteenth century to the fifteenth, when it absorbed smaller guilds, ministered, in Chambers's words, ''to the well-being of the town'' by buying masses for the dead. From the latter times, Chambers notes, ''an almost continuous register preserves the admissions of brothers and sisters, and the payment for the souls of the dead, whose masses were sung by the priests of its chapel'' (EKC 1:5).

Stratford-upon-Avon was in the parish of Stratford. The Church of the Holy Trinity being the parish church was also the place where the church court convened. The jurisdiction of the church courts covered only the goods and chattels of the dead. Chattels fell into two categories, personal and real. Within the former came household goods, money, plate, cattle, crops, and cut wood; within the latter leases and rents (Houlbrooke 90). The second level of diocesan administration comprised the archdeacons. Shakespeare's own son-in-law John Hall, named executor of the will with Susanna, his wife, served as an archdeacon at Stratford's Church of the Holy Trinity. (Also closely connected to ecclesiastical jurisdiction was one of the two trustees to whom Shakespeare and four colleagues assigned their half-share in the gardens and grounds of the Globe. When the Globe was built in 1599, "William Leveson was a churchwarden at St. Mary's, Aldermanbury . . . this was the parish of Hemmings and Condell" [Honigmann 87]).

From a contemporary of Shakespeare's, Richard Cosin, we learn of the continuing authority invested in ecclesiastical courts. According to Cosin's publication of 1593, *An Apologie of and for Sundrie Proceedings by Jurisdiction Ecclesiasticall, of late times by some challenged, and also diversly by them impugned,*[9] regarded by Houlbrooke as "the fullest and ablest defence of ecclesiastical jurisdiction written since the Reformation" (Houlbrooke in Heal & Day 256), the statutes on tithes date from the days of Richard II.

> That which is afore affirmed and determined, concerning tythes, oblations, obventions, and Mortuaries, the like is to be saide of pensions, portions, procurations, indemnities, . . . [and all] come under the jurisdiction of Ecclesiasticall persons. (15–16)

To most of the sixteenth-century population the officers of the church courts were among the most familiar representatives of authority. The ecclesiastical judges exacted when necessary the payments of tithes and offerings to the clergy, and they approved wills. Certainly Stratford-upon-Avon, situated in the rural midlands, would have been steeped in ecclesiastical custom. Dugdale gives us some idea of the ecclesiastical antiquity of the region in his record of a monastery at Stratford Church from its foundation until it was along with others in the surrounding area "dissolved, or rather swallowed up in the see and College of Worcester."

> "Some conjecture," says Leland, "that where the paroche Church is nowe, was the Monastery called Stratford given in augmentation of Evesham in St. Edwin bishop of Worcester's tyme, but the certainty of this is not knon." This was about A.D. 703. There is also some mention of a Monastery here, subordinate to Worcester, in King Berthwulf's charter, dated A.D. 845, and also in Bishop Werfrith's A.D. 872.
>
> In the 5th of Edward the IIId a College or large Chantry was founded . . . for a Warden, four Priests, three Clerks, and four Choristers, who were to celebrate divine service at the altar of St. Thomas in the south aisle (by him [John de Stratford then Bishop of Winchester, but afterward Archbishop of Canterbury] newly built) of the Parish Church of the Holy Trinity. The advowson of the Church being soon after purchased, and the

revenues of it appropriated to this College, the whole Church became Collegiate.[10]

Not only did the courts oversee matters pertaining to the ordering of the church and the clergy, but they had to be used by the laity in some of the most private matters, involving immorality, matrimonial affairs, and last wills and testaments, all of which often necessitated or resulted in massive litigation. The jurisdiction over wills and testaments held until 1857; such documents had to be proved in a church court, "in the archdeacon's or bishop's court if the property involved all lay in one diocese, in the archbishop's 'prerogative' probate court if it extended into more than one diocese."[11]

THE CLOSING STAGES OF CHANGE

During Mary's and Elizabeth's reigns the power of *Courts Christian* shifted to government, that is, taxes and levies.[12] In addition to growing hostility toward the clergy, there were attempts to curtail the power of ecclesiastical courts. In 1563 Parliament imposed stricter controls and in 1585 a bill was passed concerning the jurisdiction of these courts but Elizabeth blocked its passage (Greaves 104 ff., 674–80). The ecclesiastical courts in many cases may have been moving to protect their parishioners' holdings as well as their own, though to be sure such charity might not have been their intention. The point is that in spite of great shifts and changes in both civil and canon law, changes intended to break the back of canon law, it continued to exert the force of custom.

Interpretation of wills had been a branch of ecclesiastical jurisdiction. But by Shakespeare's day the branch of law covering the scheme of succession and testamentary matters comes, according to Holdsworth, "at the meeting place of the lay and the ecclesiastical jurisdiction":

> The common law courts, when a question of succession to moveables came before them, were apt to refer it as a matter testamentary to the practice of the ecclesiastical courts. The ecclesiastical lawyers, finding no general rules in the canon law upon these matters, were apt to refer to the common law and to the custom of the district. (*Hist Eng Law* 3:540 and 558)

And by the end of the sixteenth century and the beginning of the seventeenth, the authority of ecclesiastical courts was blocked by the common law courts in fierce rivalry over jurisdictions.

The change in the early 1600s is reflected in a noticeably rising interest in the law. There was a great increase in litigation on an unprecedented scale from the mid-sixteenth century until the outbreak of the Civil War, according to C. W. Brooks' recent study *Pettyfoggers and Vipers of the Commonwealth.*[13] The "docket rolls of prothonotaries indicate an increase of the total taken from King's Bench and Common Pleas: from 2100 in 1490 to 28,734 in 1640." In Brooks' estimation, in this period—"one of the most litigious periods in English history, if not the most"—the number of attorneys leapt from about 415 in 1580 to 1050 in 1606 (113).

The itemization of legacies of real property, that is, the minute description of items characteristic of the wills and inventories themselves, bespeaks such a growing concern. Of even greater significance, however, is the fact that among such items it was not at all uncommon to find books on both civil and canon law and on the history of English law: "Bracton appears, registers of writs, and books of the statutes" (*Hist Eng Law* 3:546). The large number of such items indicates an increasing interest in collecting the old laws, perhaps because they were becoming obsolete where they had not in fact already simply passed into custom.

RISING INTEREST IN THE LAW

In 1535, the Year Books came to an end. After two and a half centuries, the continuous stream of law reports that had been flowing since the days of Edward I became discontinuous and finally stopped. By the mid-sixteenth century, as Maitland observed, "The life of our ancient law was by no means lusty," but the latter half of the century saw a renewal of interest in ancient law. In the Inns of Court, with which Shakespeare had close connections, the Year Books were read, and other signs indicated that English law had a new lease on life. Medieval books that had been current in manuscript, many either on or about law, poured from the press in what Maitland describes as "a little Renaissance of our own: or a gothic revival if you please" (Maitland 21–22 and 29). The following monstrous list is given in its entirety to illustrate the volume of which Maitland speaks:

> In 1550 an English lawyer's library of printed books might apparently have comprised (besides some Statutes and Year Books) Littleton's Tenures, the Old Tenures, Statham's Abridgement, Fitzherbert's Abridgement, Liber Intrationum, The Old Natura Brevium, perhaps a Registrum Brevium (if that book printed in 1531, was published before 1553), Institutions or principal grounds etc. [1544], Carta feodi simplicis, [Phaer's] New book of presidentes, Diversite de courts, Novae Narrationes, Articuli ad novas narrationes, Modus tenendi curiam baronis, Modus tenendi unum hundredum, Fitzherbert's Justice of the Peace, Perkins's Profitable Book, Britton, Doctor and Student. . . . [And i]n 1600, the following might have been added: Glanvill, Bracton, Fitzherbert's Natura Brevium, Broke's Abridgement, Broke's New Cases, Rastell's Entries, Staundford's Prerogative and Pleas of the Crown, Crompton's Justice of the Peace, Crompton's Authority of Courts, West's Symbolaeography, Theloall's Digest, Smith's Commonwealth, Lambard's Archaionomia and Eirenarcha, Fulbecke's Direction or Preparative to the Study of the Law [1600], Plowden's Commentaries, Dyer's Reports and the first vol. of Coke's Reports.

William Combe, the Shakespeare family friend, had among the books in his library in Stratford *A Profitable Book of the Laws of England,* on which he had written "Cest le liver de Guilihelme Combes" and the date (1571) of his admission to the Middle Temple (Eccles 102 f.). The Renaissance interest in law may be related to what Plucknett sees as Bracton's special contribution, namely, an "ability to see through and beyond the details of procedure so as to discern the law as a series of principles." For instance, with regard to dower and its legal precedence as opposed to cases where dower must be recovered by action, Plucknett says that it marks "a fundamental step in the history of abstract thought" (51). According to Maitland, "In an age when old creeds of many kinds were crumbling and all knowledge was being transfigured . . . one body of doctrine . . . remained so intact"—the law (4).

After Edward III's Year Books came out, and from then onward, there was a flood of fourteenth-century cases coming from the sixteenth-century printers (Plucknett 112). This was largely through the initiative of Richard Tottel, who began publishing in 1553 and was prominent among publishers of law books for nearly four decades (Abbott 97). These were used almost to the exclusion of contemporary or recent cases, for the printers waited thirty or forty years before bringing out the latest cases and therefore contemporary cases were rare.

Two concurrent movements of this period, though poles apart, served as catalysts of a renewal of interest in the history of English law, and there are links between both movements and Shakespeare. The very laws and customs which we have been investigating not only were known and practiced in Shakespeare's time but were on exhibit, as it were, with singular fanfare in the revival of Anglo-Saxon customs, laws, and literature.

ENGLISH GOTHIC REVIVAL

The recusant movement was brought on by the Acts of Supremacy and Uniformity of 1559 and the further act of 1563, which, according to A. C. Southern, "required all holding, or taking, public office to subscribe to an oath forswearing the Catholic religion and denying the papal authority over the Church in England."[14] The antiquarian movement dates to 1572, when scholars interested primarily in the history of England formed the Society of Antiquaries to become pioneers in the study of Old English. Collecting and preserving the country's Anglo-Saxon heritage, antiquarians showed an increasing awareness of its submersion in the tide of change.[15] These, too, took an oath of supremacy, recognizing Elizabeth as head of the church, as Catherine Drinker Bowen observes, "to show that they contemplated nothing subversive" (*Lambarde* xii).

The publications of both groups were well known at the Inns of Court. The recusants published in Belgium and imported books on Anglo-Saxon topics and on church history. Cardinal Allen wrote to students of the Inns of Court in c. 1576 that these books "opened the way for the great Catholic revival of the 1580's" (Southern 30), two of them being Thomas Stapleton's *The History of the Church of Englande* (1565) and the great Rheims New Testament in 1582.

The four Inns of Court were the scene of further significant and revived interest in those Roman laws which formed the basis of ecclesiastical courts and Anglo-Saxon customs and laws. Several members of the Society of Antiquaries were members of one or another of these inns. Numbered among them were Matthew Parker, the leader of the movement, who later became archbishop of Canterbury; Parker's secretary John Joscelyn; William Bowyer, at one time record keeper of the Tower of London; Laurence Nowell, later the bishop of Litchfield and collector and translator of Anglo-Saxon manuscripts, his most important edition being the *Vocabularium Saxonicum* ("roughly one half of the corpus of Old English poetry" was at one time or another in Nowell's hands'' [Nowell 4]); his brother Alexander, later dean of St. Paul's; Sir Henry Spelman, who published a glossary of Latin and Anglo-Saxon law words; and the great collector Robert Cotton, at whose dwelling next door to Parliament they met.

But by far the antiquarian of most interest and significance to our present study of the laws and the will is none other than that editor of the compiled Anglo-Saxon laws in the *Archaionomia,* William Lambarde. Lambarde read law at Lincoln's Inn, and was named by Elizabeth keeper of the records in the Rolls Chapel and the Tower of London. He met Nowell in London when the latter was staying at one period in the chambers of his brother, Robert Nowell, attorney-general of the Court of Wards, in Gray's Inn (*DNB* 696), and with Nowell was one of the pioneers in the study of Old English; indeed, Nowell quite inexplicably in 1567 simply turned over all his manuscripts and all his work to be carried on by Lambarde.

SHAKESPEARE'S PERSONAL KNOWLEDGE OF THE OLD LAWS

For proof of Shakespeare's personal knowledge of the laws, one would of course first think of the most likely place, the plays. But this approach would yield little success, for the plays contain no direct allusions to the specific laws I have shown to be operative in the will. They are not to be our source for the poet's personal knowledge of the civil and ecclesiastical laws that give us a new basis for interpretation of the will. It is in works produced by the two movements of the English Gothic Revival that such evidence is to be found.

In the reign of Henry I the laws of Canute were ''given the place of honour by the Latin writers who translated and made compilations of the Anglo-Saxon codes and wrote treatises of the law,'' as Professor Whitelock points out. A few changes had been introduced by William I, the most notable in terms of the legal intricacies of Shakespeare's will being ''a sharper differentiation between ecclesiastical and lay courts'' (*HLL* 6:27).

The two most comprehensive manuscripts of the Anglo-Saxon laws were compiled in Henry's reign, namely the *Textus Roffensis* (which will be of interest with regard to Shakespeare's knowledge of these laws), and the St. Paul's manuscript now in Corpus Christi College, Cambridge (*HLL* 6:27).

However, one of the very best codifications of the early laws, as it turns out, is also our very best source of evidence for making a strong case that Shakespeare not only knew of such laws but may have counted among his personal library a collection of them. If the signature "Wm Shakspere" on the Folger Library's copy of William Lambarde's *Archaionomia* (see Figure 4) be that of the poet—and it is now considered highly likely[16]—then he had in his possession parallel texts in Anglo-Saxon and Latin of the "laws from Ine to Canute, inclusive, and the 'Canones Aelfrici.' " This compilation confirms the two legalities related to reparation and reconciliation extensively treated in Chapter Four.

The *Archaionomia,* considered by R. J. Schoeck "a pioneer work in restoring the forgotten laws to the students of the common law,"[17] was William Lambarde's publication of the laws transcribed by Laurence Nowell, collector and translator of Anglo-Saxon manuscripts, with the addition of a parallel Latin translation. To Nowell's *Vocabularium Saxonicum* Lambarde added several legal terms: "Thirty of the thirty-six specific references to the Old English legal codes which appear in the *Vocabularium* are in Lambarde's handwriting."[18]

Giles E. Dawson, then chief paleographer of the Folger Library and discoverer of the signature, wrote an account of the acquisition of the book and subsequent discovery of the signature in which he concludes that "W. S. wrote his signature on this title page, perhaps because he owned the book—a strange volume indeed for his library."[19] Schoenbaum, too, regards the book as "an odd choice for Shakespeare's library," and will not go so far as to say that it offers definite proof that Shakespeare was during the "lost years" a lawyer's scrivener (*Rec & Images* 108–9).

It is possible that the book served Shakespeare's interests in the suit he started in Chancery Court in 1578 for the recovery of the Asbies property, land his mother had inherited from her father but mortgaged to her brother-in-law when she and Shakespeare's father were in financial straits. Though the suit was unsuccessful (Alexander 101), in *Archaionomia* "freehold," that is, hereditary property, is discussed under "Bocland," that is, "folkland" or hereditary property (Dii). In this connection the Society's investigations of the College of Heralds and titles of honour may also have had some bearing on John Shakespeare's renewal of his application for a coat of arms, which was approved by Garter King-at-Arms in 1596, only a few months before Shakespeare purchased New Place in Stratford.

The book, the first Anglo-Saxon text to appear in print, was printed in London by John Day, as Dunkel has pointed out in *Lambarde,* "a

ΑΡΧΑΙΟΝΟΜΙΑ,
SIVE
de priscis anglorum legibus libri, sermone Anglico, vetustate antiquissimo, aliquot abhinc seculis conscripti, atq; nunc demum, magno iurisperitorum, & amantium antiquitatis omnium commodo, è tenebris in lucem vocati.
Gulielmo Lambardo interprete.
Regum qui has Leges scripserunt nomenclationem, & quid praeterea accesserit, altera monstrabit pagina.
LONDINI,
ex officina Joannis Daij.
An. 1568.
CVM GRATIA ET PRIVILEGIO
Regiae Maiestatis per Decennium.

In hoc opere continentur,

Leges { Inæ, Occiduorum Saxonum Regis. 1
Aluredi, totius Angliæ Regis. 19

Figure 4 **The Signature on the Title Page of Lambarde's *Archaionomia*, from *Rec & Images* 105–6. By permission of the Folger Shakespeare Library.**

well-known printer of books by Protestant divines,'' and was ''avidly searched for precedents'' by common lawyers in the seventeenth century.[20] Indeed, its importance as a source of legal history continues to be recognized even though scholarship of our day has uncovered many errors in the Anglo-Saxon transcription (see Kenneth Sisam on the specific errors and Elizabethan renderings of the Old English supplied by Nowell and/or Lambarde, ''not with intention to deceive,'' in *Studies in the History of Old English Literature* 232–58).

In the prefatory commentary, which bears the date 1568, Lambarde makes special reference to his rendering of Anglo-Saxon *cyricsceatte* into Latin *primitiae seminum,* as in its first appearance in the Laws of Ine.[21]

> Be cyric ſceatte.
> Cẏric ſceattas sẏn aʒiſene be
> Seint martynes maeſſan; Giſ hwa
> ꝥ ne ʒelæste. ſẏ he ſcyldiʒ
> ſeowertiʒ ſcill. ⁊be twelſſe ldum
> aʒyſe ðone cyricſceat; (Cii^{V})
> De primitiis Seminum.
> Primitiae seminum ad celebre divi
> Martini festured duntor, qui tum no
> solverit, 40 solidis mulctator, &
> ipsas preterea primitias duodecies
> persolvito. (Ciii)

> [Concerning churchshot. Churchshot is to be rendered by Saint Martin's Mass. Anyone who has not carried out payment by this day is liable for [or fined] 60 shillings [the Latin solidus is the equivalent of 12 denarii, each denarius equivalent to 5 shillings, hence = 60 shillings] and required to render it twelvefold (my translation).]

In the same opening section, entitled ''Rerum & verborum/Explicatio'' (Di), Shakespeare would have found a glossary of the very terms we have been reviewing. Albert H. Marckwardt, editor of Nowell's *Vocabularium,* posits that this glossary ''may be considered the finest printed nucleus of an Old English vocabulary'' (14). If the copy did belong to Shakespeare, one might assume that he was capable of the Latin at least and perhaps dare to deduce that he was at least familiar with Anglo-Saxon. The language of the entries in the *Archaionomia* may appear curious because of the Law French used. ''The language of English jurisprudence until the fifteenth century,'' we are informed by Mark Edwin Andrews (17), Law French was a mixture of the Latin of Julius Caesar, the French of William the Conqueror, and the English of Chaucer.

Heriot is listed in the glossary before churchshot and scot:

Heryot. Hereotum, Saxonicè hereȝeat vocabulum ab bere (quod exercitum sonat) effictum, atque armamenta, sive belli instrumenta significat. Constat sanè Hereotum his primis temporibus nomine apparatus bellici dominis tributum, id quod etiam nunc aliquibus in locis observatur. Datur quidem & hodie passim Hereotum, sed longè ab hoc nostro diversum. Immo quod hac nostra memoria Gallicè relief dicitur, veteris illius hereotivim obtinet. Conjectura est igitur, Normanos victores Anglis victis, omnia spoliatis armatura, heriotum remisisse atq̃ a miseris pecuniam exigisse. (Biiii^{V})

[Heriot signifies ships' gear or instruments of war. It is certain absolutely that heriot from the first times referred to the equipment of war that was a tribute to the lord, the thing which is still now observed in some places in this way, that heriot is given at any rate today here and there, but long since in our different ways. I think that in this our memory of relief from the Gauls is spoken of, that tradition from which heriot is derived. There is therefore a conjectural inference that the Normans after conquering the English and stripping them of all armor, restored to them the heriot but demanded money from the poor. (My translation.)]

Cyricsceat. Primitiae seminum Saxonicè Cyricsceat, ad verbum vectigal ecclesiasticum. Hic videntur justae interpretationis loco verba ex veteri quodam legum libello desumpta, digna quae subjiciantur. Ibi autem legitur ad hunc modum, Chircheseed, ou Chirceomer, ou Chirceamber, suit un certein de blee batu, que chescun home devoit al temps dez Brytons, & dez Engles, porter a lour esglise le jour Seint Marten. Id si verum sit, constat falsò scribî cyricſceat pro cyricſaed; ſaed etenim apud illos semen significat, sceat vero (unde id quod vulgò Shot) pecuniam sive vectigal sonat. (Di)

[First fruit in Saxon churchscot, according to the ecclesiastical word of tithe. Here the words chosen from a certain old small book of law seem of the right interpretation, and they are worthy to have the same meaning; however, in that place, it was written in this manner, Chirchseed, or Chirceomer, or Chirceamber, derived from a certain amount of beaten or refined wheat, that each man was obliged during the time of the Britons and the Angles, to carry to his church in the day of Saint Martin. If that were true, it is wrong to write cyricsceat for cyricsaed; sead as a matter of fact in their writings means seed [offspring, race by association]. Whereas sceat (from which the vulgar form Shot comes) means money or tithe. (My translation).]

Scata, vocabulum a Saxonico Sceatta effictum, Est autem Sceatta ingens argenti summa. quippe quae argenti quinque millia contineat. (Di^V)
[Scot, a word derived from the Saxon Sceatta, (tribute), but Sceatta is a vast sum of money if one's holdings are up to five thousand. (My translation)]

Once into the text of laws themselves, Shakespeare would have found a passage in the laws of Edmund where both tithes (''teoðunȝum'') of ''cyric sceatum'' and ''aelmes seoh'' are cited (Xi^V). It is clearly shown that whoever did not pay them was held in extreme disrepute (''qui non solverit, anathema esto''). And in the laws of Edgar for the first time a clear distinction is made between tithes and churchscot: (churchscot as second law, tithes as third law) (Yi^V–Yii).

The laws of Canute, so important for containing early references to soul-scot, comprise the last section of Lambarde's compilation. Martinmas is still cited as the day when churchshot is due (10, $Eeiii^V$), and Canute also orders the due of heriot (hereȝeate) ($Kkiiii^V$–Lli).

And sawlsceat is rihtaest *t*oman rẏmle ȝelaeste â æt openum ȝraefe. Yȝif man aeniȝ lic ofriht scrẏft scine elleshwære lecȝe. ȝelaeste ðam mynstre ðe hitto hynde. ($Eeiii^V$)
Atque si quis extra suae paroeciae fines mortuum humarit aliquem, ipsa nihilo secius pecunia sepulcralis Ecclesiae (ad quam jure pertineat) redditor. (Eeiiii)

[And it is best that payment for the souls of the dead should always be rendered at the open grave. Likewise if one had to bury a dead person outside the limits of his parish nothing but the same burial dues of the sepulchral Church (to which they belong by right) let him pay back.]

The Society of Antiquaries was dissolved by King James in 1614, because they were not providing evidence for his divine right theory. They showed that English law and precedent distributed power equally among the king, the nobility, and the commons (Dunkel xvii–xii, 27–28). As a result of the antiquaries' efforts, we may say with certainty that the law which seems to have been the archetype of the second best formula—and which, as I shall show in the following chapter, was used widely in medieval and Elizabethan wills—was not only known in Shakespeare's time but was even appearing in current printed editions.

THE RECUSANTS

Shakespeare and other members of his family may also have known firsthand of the recusants, the other group involved in the revival of interest in ecclesiastical laws. There is interesting evidence that John Shakespeare, the poet's father, was of the Catholic recusancy. Peter Milward, S. J., cites one "item of information which places the matter beyond reasonable doubt," that is, the discovery of a copy of "a Spiritual Testament, or profession of adherence to the Catholic faith, composed by St. Charles Borromeo" and "drawn up in the name of John Shakespeare." The discovery of this document in 1757 by a bricklayer working on Shakespeare's birthplace in Henley Street has of course stirred up considerable controversy, as being a possible forgery typical of that period. However, in the past fifty years, as other copies of the Spiritual Testament have been uncovered, its authenticity has become more widely accepted. Milward also offers evidence that Shakespeare's maternal religious background was Catholic and recusant; he further points out that an Isabella and a Joan Shakespeare were prioress and subprioress, respectively, of the convent at Wroxhall, from whose neighborhood "the forbears of John Shakespeare seem to have come."[22] George Keeton argues that the famous deer poaching incident involving Sir Thomas Lucy was really a recusant situation. Lucy had no park from which the young Shakespeare could steal deer, but "as Lord-Lieutenant it was his duty to enforce the laws against recusants, and in 1583 the kin of Shakespeare's mother were distantly implicated in a Catholic plot." Lucy was instructed by the Council to order the arrest of the suspected persons. The events of 1583 may have touched Shakespeare and may also have been responsible for his flight to London (Keeton 100). Further evidence for Shakespeare's Catholic ties may be seen in the citation of Susanna Shakespeare Hall in 1606 in a list of recusants at Stratford, pointed out by E.A.J. Honigmann in *Shakespeare: The "Lost Years"*[23], a list which included two whose names were bracketed with John Shakespeare " 'included in a return for recusancy in 1592' " (Hanley 441), and further in his links to the Lancastrian Catholic families of Hoghton and Hesketh, and to other loyal recusant Lancastrian connections like John Cottom, retired Stratford schoolmaster, whose brother, Thomas, was captured and arraigned along with the Jesuit Edmund Campion in 1582 (Honigmann 5, 114–15), and John Weever, poet, who apparently had ties with Sir Robert Cotton, whom he described as "the only repairer of ruined antiquity" (Honigmann 80–81). Peter Levi tells us that William Reynolds, named in the will, was raised by parents who had been Catholics and harbored Jesuits (Levi 341).

Thus it appears likely that Shakespeare personally was closely connected, both in his immediate Stratford family circle and in the London of the Inns of Court and the antiquarians, to those of his time most involved in the study and/or revival of ancient laws. His ties with ecclesiastical courts where the old laws had held sway for so long are even more extensive.

ECCLESIASTICAL COURTS, THE SHAKESPEARES, AND THE HATHAWAYS

Shakespeare's father has been identified as John of Snitterfield, who administered the estate of Richard Shakespeare (presumably his father) in 1561.[24] As alderman and high bailiff of Stratford, John Shakespeare would have known of all the ecclesiastical polity.[25]

And if Anne is the Anne Hathaway who was born in 1556 of Richard and Joan Hathaway of Shottery at Hewland, then it is from ecclesiastical court records similar to the kind that will prove so elucidating in the present study of Shakespeare's will that recent research has learned so much about her.

One cannot overstate the importance of this field of study. These historical records of the Church Court, or "Bawdy Court" as it was generally called, have remained almost wholly unexplored. E. R. C. Brinkworth, a pioneer in the field, affirms G. R. Elton's observation in *England, 1200–1640: The Sources of History* on their potentialities to "illuminate the history of church and people in ways which no other source can. They take one to the realities."[26]

With regard to the Worcester Consistory Court, Gray found from examining the act and deposition books—the records of proceedings—that it was formerly held at the western end of the south aisle of the cathedral and that in Shakespeare's day Dr. Cosin was the judge, to whom matters concerning testamentary, matrimonial, tithe, and defamation cases were submitted, "the depositions containing much interesting matter relating to the counties of Warwick and Worcester, with many references to names of persons and places well known in connection with the

Shakespeare families'' (208–9). The volume covering the period of Shakespeare's early life has been lost.

The Stratford court records are preserved in two act books, the first covering the years 1590–1616 and the second covering 1622–1624. In surveying them, Brinkworth found an interesting entry that shows how such records shed light on the history of people and form a kind of continuity from generation to generation. In January 1622–23, George Robbins and Oliver Sandells were cited for playing cards during Evening Prayer time. As Brinkworth points out, ''Sandells was a son of Fulke Sandells, the friend of Shakespeare's youth who in 1582 was one of the sureties for his marriage bond at Worcester. The year before that he was an overseer of Richard Hathaway's will and answerable for paying Anne Hathaway £6 13s.4d. on the day she married'' (Brinkworth 55–56).

Church records have been the source of information pertaining to Shakespeare and Anne's marriage and to their children. Records indicate the marriage license was issued in 1582 by the Bishop of Worcester in whose diocese Stratford is located (Bentley 29). The clerk noted Anne Whateley of Temple Grafton, ''but this is pretty surely a mistake'' (Bentley 31). The marriage license was issued by the Bishop of Worcester, though it is not known exactly where the wedding took place (*Doc Life* 71–72). It was definitely not in the Stratford parish church, giving rise to much suggestive speculation, especially since their first child was born only six months later. However, the matrimonial customs of the times might help to remove the stigma of the situation. As Marchette Chute points out, pre-contracts were ''taken seriously'' by Elizabethan church law; Shakespeare's own maternal aunt, Agnes Arden, was referred to in her father's will as the wife of Thomas Stringer even though she did not marry him until the following October. In Shakespeare's case the bond of November 28 was posted to indemnify the court should objections to the marriage arise later. And the license was required because it was during ''prohibited season'' between Advent and the octave of the Epiphany. They would have had to wait until January, and apparently she was already pregnant. However, there is no reason to suppose it was necessarily a stealthy affair, because they could not have taken out a license without the approval of Shakespeare's father (20–23). Swinburne is our best source on the matter; in his *A Treatise of Spousals, or Matrimonial Contracts; Wherein All the Questions relating to that Subject are ingeniously Debated and Resolved* (1606, 1686), he differentiates between ''spousals'' and ''solemnizing,'' citing the usually recognized solemnity of marriage whether or not banns are published (a subject treated at more length with full quotation in Chapter Five, p. 174 f.), and further he declares the "ripe or lawful age" at which matrimony may be contracted: for the man, fourteen, for the woman, twelve.[27]

The child, Susanna, was accorded full, perhaps even special, ecclesiastical approbation, for she was christened on May 26, 1583, on Trinity Sunday, the feast day of Holy Trinity Church (see Figure 5). The fact that her grandfather was John Shakespeare, alderman, could not have been without its influence. Schoenbaum's examination of the parish register led him to conclude that her name was one "appealing to" Puritans "but still rather novel in Stratford, first appearing in the parish register in 1574"; in April, right before Susanna Shakespeare's christening, two other babies named Susanna were also christened (*Doc Life* 76). The parish register records less than two years later the christening of the Shakespeares' twins, Hamnet and Judith, on February 2, 1585, named after the family's neighbors and lifelong friends, Hamnet and Judith Sadler. Thus by 1585, when he was almost twenty-one and she twenty-eight, Shakespeare had a wife and three children.

Much later, ecclesiastical court records figure into family history again, when Susanna's name appears in a consistory scandal case in which she was accused of adultery and later brought action for defamation against John Lane. John Lane did not appear in court and was excommunicated. It has been claimed that the lawyer who represented Susanna Hall was Robert Whattcott, one of the witnesses of the dramatist's will (Knight 254).

Church records have also been found concerning Judith's husband, Thomas, "sonne to Richard Queeny," a friend of Shakespeare. The Shakespeare–Quiney family friendship went back to John Shakespeare and Adrian Quiney. Both Judith and Thomas were baptized in February, but he in 1588–89. Their marriage ceremony took place on February 10, 1616, during the Lenten prohibited season (probably on account of her pregnancy, as mentioned before) which, in 1616, according to Schoenbaum, began on January 28 and ended on April 7. They were therefore required to have a special license, but because they did not, were cited in consistory court in Worcester Cathedral (*Doc Life* 239). They did not show up. They were summoned again but stayed away a second time. On March 12, Thomas was excommunicated (there is no record that Judith was), but apparently the excommunication "was the result of a dispute between the Bishop's Court and the Vicar's Court for

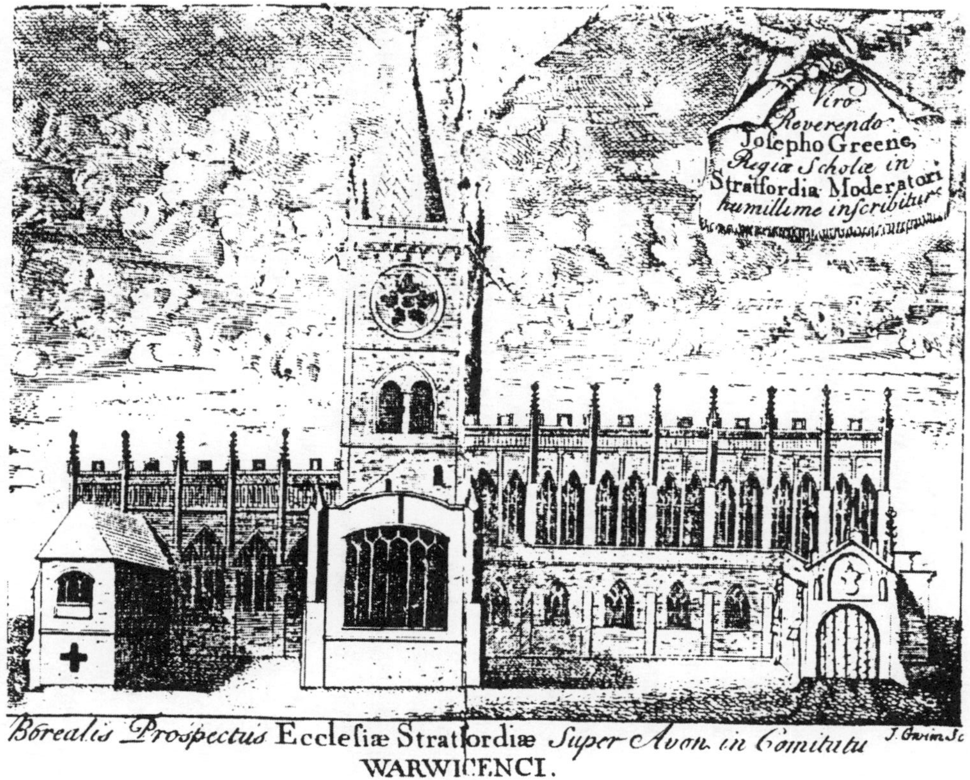

Figure 5 Holy Trinity Church at the Time of Shakespeare. From Patricia Wainwright, *Trinity Tales: Some Lesser Known Stories of Shakespeare's Church* (Holy Trinity, Stratford-upon-Avon: The Parochial Church Council, 1983).

which he [Quiney] could hardly be held responsible by Shakespeare'' (Hanley 441). Apparently, the controversy was over who had the right that year to issue marriage licenses. The excommunication was short-lived, since on November 23, 1616, only eight months later, a first child, a boy whom they named ''Shakspere,'' was christened in Stratford Church just four days from what would have been Shakespeare and Anne's thirty-fourth anniversary. Unfortunately, Shakspere Quiney did not survive his sixth-month birthday, dying May 18, 1617.

Church records, specifically the Vicar's Court at Maidstone (Hanley 441), are the source of our knowledge of the other crisis of the same period involving this couple, namely, Quiney's having gotten another woman pregnant before marrying Judith and the deaths of the woman and her baby in childbirth—their burials were dated March 15, 1616. On March 26, one day after the date of the final draft of Shakespeare's will, Quiney was heard by the ecclesiastical court, where he was charged with ''incontinence with a certain Margaret Wheelar [sic]'' and was sentenced to public penance clothed in a sheet for three Sundays in said church of Stratford (Hanley 441). However, Quiney paid 5 shillings and requested penance be remitted, so he was dismissed. The ecclesiastical court records apprise us of the fact that Judith and her husband suffered the deaths of all their children, two sons having been born after little Shakspere, in 1618 and 1620, both dying in the same year, 1639 (Eccles 140).

The records also show Anne's family as having been much involved in church affairs, but not in court cases. Her brother Bartholomew was sworn in on April 13, 1608, as a church warden, that is, as representative of the local community in its ecclesiastical affairs, performing important duties, such as administering parish funds, keeping up the fabric and furniture of the church, and responding to the bishop or the archdeacon concerning parish morals or affairs (Rodes 162). His son John followed his father in the office and ''first took his oath at Easter-tide 1616, only a few days before the death of his uncle'' (Brinkworth 22 ff.). Mutschmann and Wentersdorf give the son's name as having been Richard (195); Richard was a baker in Stratford. In the Chipping Norton Register of *Berk's Oxon &c,* a brief manuscript of miscellany, such as baptisms, there is an entry for 1603, ''Richard Hathaway was vicar,'' but by 1607 he had been replaced by one Edward Allaway.

The ecclesiastical courts are a source which scholars have only begun to mine as are the laws of the time in general.[28] We have seen how profitable a reexamination of laws has been with regards to gaining a new insight into the concerns of the poet's will. Darryl Gless has brought out the importance of sixteenth-century religious law in his interpretation of *Measure for Measure,*[29] and Margaret Loftus Ranald has shown how Renaissance marriage laws can serve to clarify otherwise obscure points in the plays.

Shakespeare's will is a register of these predominantly legal interests of his day. Also, the people involved in the making of it had notable legal ties. With the exception of family and actor friends, most of the others named in the will or witnessing to it had some connection with law. Thomas Russell, one of those named to be overseer, was an Alderminster squire (*Doc Life* 247), who was son of Sir Thomas Russell and educated at Queen's College, Oxford.[30] Leonard Digges, who contributed a commendatory poem to the First Folio of the plays, was his stepson (Hotson 214). Francis Collins was a lawyer, about to be appointed town clerk of Stratford. Julius Shaw was high bailiff of Stratford and an alderman; Whattcott was a lawyer; Thomas Combe's brother studied at the Middle Temple; Walker's father was an alderman; and even the house in which the poet lived his last years, New Place, had been purchased from a lawyer (Knight 269–70).

That there were ties between Shakespeare and the old laws we have been examining can hardly be doubted, in light of what we have learned of his probable intimate knowledge of them and the legal contexts of the times in which the will was drafted.

The interesting and ironic thing is that we owe what knowledge we have of these meanings to the efforts of a few of Shakespeare's contemporaries, who collected and preserved the laws and literature of England's past for future generations. Their work enables us today to trace the history of the medieval institutions of heriots and mortuaries to their religious origins and unearth a meaning for the phrase "second best" which renders that bequest in many ways the most poignant of all the legacies in the will.

Chapter Four

The Will as Religious Testament

"Item I gyve unto my wief my second best bed with the furniture."

There was never much more than passing interest in Shakespeare's interlineated provision to his wife until Edmond Malone provided an accurate text for it, replacing what had long been the reading of "*brown* best bed," with "*second* best bed," the "furniture" referring to "the bed furnishings," such as hangings and so on (*Sh's Lives* 182). Until then, there had been little concern over the fact that the bequest was a bed, or that this was the only named bequest to his wife, or even that it was interlineated and by implication merely an afterthought. Since Malone's discovery, however, as Schoenbaum tersely observes, this infamous interlineation has been the center of "endless, mostly unprofitable, controversy" (*Doc Life* 247), either maliciously enjoyed as a slur or protectively defended as a sign of affection.

As Schoenbaum sums it up in *Shakespeare's Lives,* essentially there are two opposing views: one, that Shakespeare knew his wife would be provided for by dower right and that the bed was probably of sentimental value to them, possibly, in Leslie Steevens' opinion, even "the bridal bed,"[1] and the other, summed up in the very influential retort made by Edmond Malone in his reconstruction of the events surrounding the will, that the fact that it is only an interlineation in the will shows that Shakespeare "had forgot her,—he had recollected her,—but so recollected her, as more strongly to mark how little he esteemed her; he had already (as is vulgarly expressed) cut her off, not indeed with a shilling, but with an old bed."[2]

The discovery of similar bequests in wills of the period, pointed out by C. Knight in the last century,[3] seemed to offer some hope of clarification but in fact has done little toward settling the matter since it can be used to strengthen the position of either side, depending upon the specific wording of the will. For example, Schoenbaum in *Shakespeare's Lives* notes Boswell's find among Malone's *Adversaria* of the will of Sir Thomas Lucy the younger, who in 1600 left his second son, Richard, his "second-best horse, but no land" (247), a bequest which can be read as suggesting rather less than more affection in the remembrance, and quotes Halliwell-Phillipps' conclusions that the second best bed "was the usual mode of expressing a mark of great affection" (409).

One particularly good example supporting the affectionate reading was brought forward by Mark Eccles. William Palmer of Leamington, 1573, left his wife, Elizabeth, "all hir wearing apparell" and his "second best fetherbed for hir selfe furnished, And one other meaner fetherbed furnished for hir mayde . . . And that I wolde have hir to live as one that were and had bien my wief" (Eccles 164–65). By comparison to what Eccles describes as such "conjugal tenderness," Schoenbaum concludes that "the scant attention paid to the spouse" in Shakespeare's will "is unusual" and also takes note of the absence of expressions "of testamentary emotion," but he suggests that "perhaps his lawyer did not encourage, or permit, such embellishments" (*Doc Life* 248).

The example from Palmer's will certainly convinces one that the bequest was "an affectionate gesture towards a cherished spouse," as Schoenbaum expresses it (*Sh's Lives* 742). But then the wording of the will is quite explicit here, too. And the question remains, is Shakespeare's interlineation meant as a sign of affection or contempt?

My investigation into the origins of the term led me to believe that the problem lies in our understanding of the term "second best." The assumption has been that there are no alternative meanings to the familiar one denoting a quality of being inferior to, "not so good as." If the inferiority is ascribed to Anne, the inference has extended by association to their entire relationship or Shakespeare's opinion of it. If to an actual bed, then the possibilities are countless, depending upon what can be uncovered about all the beds in the Shakespeare household, or about the significance or sentiment attached to those beds, or even about the social customs that prevailed in the Stratford of that time.

But the alternative meaning of "second best" that I propose is derived from my study of ecclesiastical law, presented in the preceding chapter, and this meaning is related to the religious nature of the medieval will. As Lambarde's collection of the ancient laws in the *Archaion-*

omia reveals, a meaning for "second best" was as many centuries old in use prior to the sixteenth century as in disuse since that time. The historical origins and uses made of the formula "second best" support an affectionate reading of the phrase. At the same time it introduces a dimension of meaning to the term which, though new to us, would not have been unfamiliar to most of those living in Elizabethan England.

The customary use of the phrase "second best" may be taken as evidence for its having been a term of a singular significance, derived from centuries of ecclesiastical tradition. From a strictly canonical usage in an ancient law of tithe, the term "second best" appears to have passed into custom as a metaphorical formula conveying essentially the same meanings it had always had. By using the term, a man could make certain acknowledgments that would, he hoped, settle something in his soul.

SECOND BEST AND THE SOUL'S SALVATION: THE HEIR-LOOM

The religious nature of the medieval will is its essence. It is rooted in Anglo-Saxon Christian funerary practice. "Both literary and legal scholars are agreed that the will of the sixteenth century was inherently, essentially, fundamentally and organizationally Anglo-Saxon" (BRL 2: 474). In spite of the fact that by Shakespeare's time civil law had usurped the authority of ecclesiastical courts, or *Courts Christian* as they were also called, the will—as twentieth-century legal historians Sir Frederick Pollock and Frederic William Maitland emphatically state—"is still a religious instrument made in the name of the Father, Son and Holy Ghost. The testator's first thought is not of the transmission of an *hereditas,* but of the future welfare of his immortal soul and his mortal body" (Pol & Mait 338).

The religious character of the will is apparent in the rhetoric of testamentary writing, in particular the Roman form of wills, a form, B. Roland Lewis claims, most often used by Christians. According to Lewis, the first section of this form, designated the *notificatio* ("identification of the person and notification of the intent of a testator"), was "in the nature of an oath. The making of a will was a serious matter—a holy act" (BRL 2: 482).[4] The form, following the exordium in the notification, "ffirst I Comend my Soule," etc., was the formula of wills of the Elizabethan period, and though some have regarded it as indicative of sectarian faith, in Schoenbaum's view such "confidence is misplaced:

testators, whether Catholics or Protestants, could use the same exordium without . . . regarding it as an avowal of sectarian faith'' (*Comp Doc Life* 59). Shakespeare's will follows this form:

> In the name of god Amen I William Shackspeare of Stratford vpon Avon in the countie of Warr gent in perfect health & memorie god be praysed doe make & Ordayne this my last will & testament in manner & forme followeing That ys to saye ffirst I Comend my Soule into the handes of god my Creator hoping & assuredlie beleeving through thonelie merittes of Jesus Christe my Saviour to be made partaker of lyfe everlastinge And my bodye to the Earth whereof yt ys made. (See Figure 1)[5]

The seriousness of attitude is demonstrated by a concomitant feature of medieval wills, that is, the frequency and intensity of curses that were either incorporated into the will proper or, as in Shakespeare's case, set out as epitaphs on tombstones. The reader should also take note of the *cwide* or *quides* (oral statements) alluded to in the curses as it is to them that B. Roland Lewis traces the heritage of the Elizabethan will (BRL 2:474).

Out of the thirty-nine wills included in Dorothy Whitelock's collection of Anglo-Saxon wills, twenty-one incorporate curses similar to the following:

> And swa hwile man swa þisne cwide
> awende, sy he Iudas gefere ðe urne
> drihten belewde on helle wite.
>
> [And whatsoever man shall alter this bequest, may he be a companion in the torment of hell of Judas who betrayed our Lord.] (66–67)

> And wo so þis quides berenen wille,
> berene hym god heueriche, buten he
> it her bete.
>
> [And whosoever wishes to despoil this will, may God deprive him of the Kingdom of heaven, unless he repent it here.] (70–71)

Shakespeare's epitaph by comparison seems rather tame.

> Good Frend for Jesus sake Forbeare,
>
> To Digg the Dust Encloased Heare,

Bleste Be $\overset{e}{\text{y}}$ Man $\overset{T}{\text{y}}$ Spares Thes Stones,
And Curst Be He $\overset{T}{\text{y}}$ Moves My Bones.

(*Doc Life* 250)

Yet, Anne certainly took it very seriously; in settling upon her own gravesite, she respected his wishes rather than bring a cruse on herself in spite of her fervent desire to be laid to rest with him in his grave.

For several centuries the English will retained the character of its original introduction into England, that is, as pointed out by Michael Sheehen in his very fine study *The Will in Medieval England from the Conversion of the Anglo-Saxons to the End of the Thirteenth Century,* it remained an instrument for the giving of alms (303). Sheehan thus confirms the notion of the medieval English will as "an act characterized by religious solicitude. Provisions for the future of the soul, payment of debt, and rectification of the injustices of the past were usually its chief concern" (258).

Bequests, too, developed out of the fundamental concern with provision. From the earliest primitive type of personal bequest, the practice became more pronounced, ultimately becoming a distinguishing feature of the medieval will. The legacy of heirlooms was derived from a form that appeared in the very first kinds of wills, largely of the *healme and heorðe* variety, according to Dorothy Whitelock, an alliterative formula which referred to the whole homestead, including both dwelling place and cultivated land. The "healm" stubble refers to the fields from which the harvest was garnered (*Eng Hist Doc* 1: n. 1, 406). As Professor Whitelock explains, the reservation of certain chattels for the use of the heir became the *principalia,* the tools of the heir, or "heir-looms" (*Eng Hist Doc* 1:371). Heirlooms are goods and personal chattels that by special custom went "to the heir along with the inheritance" (Blackstone II, ch. 28, 427).

The term *loom,* Blackstone tells us, is Saxon in origin, and signified a limb or a member, "so that an heirloom is nothing else, but a limb or member of the inheritance," the general custom regarding an heirloom as something that "cannot be taken away without damaging or dismembering the freehold," or as being unable to "be severed from thence without violence or damage, such as marble chimney-pieces, benches, and the like" (*Commentaries* 427: Blackstone adds that the same law was observed in France and Venice). Or it may have been something of special value, as Sheehan brings out: "[O]ften the best example of each type of chattel [household equipment, tools for farmwork or for trade] was set apart as an heirloom" (*Will Med Eng* 295). At any rate, heirlooms eventually came to be individually specified in the more recent type of testament.

As Pollock and Maitland point out, "The medieval will is characterized by the large number of its specific bequests. The horses are given away one by one; so are the jewels; so are the beds and quilts, the pots and pans" (*Pol & Mait* 338–39). Examples from *Lincoln Wills* provide an especially fascinating array of such bequests: "a horse called Begger," mares named Broke and Mope, stalls of bees and beehives, a red "nyght bonnet," a gown of Bruges satin, cups, nuts, goblets, apostle-spoons (*OED:* "old fashioned silver spoons, the handles of which end in figures of the Apostles, with the proper ensign; the usual present of sponsors at baptism; also 'spoons with the postells,' "),[6] buckles, and a girdle "dymysyn gylt with a rede stone and vj perels (apparels) and the coorse rasyd warke" (2: xxiv). Others of such "smaller legacies of former days," as cited by Halliwell-Phillipps, are kettles, chairs, gowns, hats, eather bolsters, and cullenders (H–P, *Life* 177).

In addition to the array of specific legacies, another remarkable feature of bequests in medieval wills, one of particular interest with regard to the bequest in question here, is the widespread practice of differentiation between best and second best bequests. This is truly a fascinating feature since it appears in wills not only of earlier date but also from various geographical areas, and what is even more remarkable, the expression "second best" is used in connection with all sorts of items other than beds.

For example, Furnivall's *The Fifty Earliest English Wills* (1882) includes one from 1439: "To Watkyn Asshwell my secunde best furre and gowne."[7] In a will made in 1600 the younger Sir Thomas Lucy of Charlecote devised to his second son, Richard, "my second-best horse and furnyture," but no land, "because this his father-in-law had already promised him" (*SL* 247); and in a will of 1621 Bartholomew Hathaway left to his son Edmund "my second brass pott" (H-P, *Outlines* 259). In his will of 1521, Richard Marley simply differentiated between best and any other, bequeathing to his son Crystofe "my best fetherbed with my best trannson two of my best pillowes thre peyer of my best shetes my best covett with my best hangyng aboute my bedd" (*Test Papers* 2:6–7).

These wills, like Shakespeare's, demonstrate the medieval will's emphasis upon specific legacies of movables as well as an established distinction between best and second best. As I pointed out at the beginning of this chapter, the large number of such incidences of similar bequests of a bed was the basis for conclusions that it was not a rare occurrence, and certainly not unique. Hall's *Testamentary Papers II* includes a will of December 22, 1608, in which Thomas Combe left all bedsteads to his wife "except the best," which "with the best Bedd and best furniture thereunto belonging" was left to his son William.[8] In the April 1610 will of John Harris, a well-to-do notary of Lincoln, he left his wife "a freehold estate and other property," but also bequeathed to her "the standing bedstead in the litle chaumber, *with the second-best featherbed I have, with a whole furniture therto belonging* [my italics], and allso a trundle-bedsted with a featherbed, and the furniture therto belonging and six payer of sheetes, three payer of the better sorte and three payer of the meaner sorte" (H-P, *Outlines* 259). Here, of course, she gets both beds, and more. What is apparent is the distinction made in who were to be the best and second best inheritors.

Emmison concluded, "After reading all the Essex wills of the period, that at least a hundred use the identical or a similar phrase in relation to the wife. It is the eldest son, not the widow, who usually gets the best bed" (31). As mentioned above, Halliwell-Phillipps, in *The Life of William Shakespeare,* held that the first-best bed was "that generally reserved for visitors, and one which may possibly have descended as a family heirloom, becoming in that way the undevisable property of his eldest daughter. Bedsteads were sometimes of elaborate workmanship, and gifts of them are often to be met with in ancient wills" (177). This interest both in specific bequests and their designation in terms of "best" and "second best" appear even in late records as for example in Chief Justice Coke's *Commentarie Upon Littleton* (1629 ed.): "And note that, in some places, chattels as heirloomes, as the *best bed,* table, pot, pan, cart, and other dead chattels moveable, may go to the heire, and the heire in that case may have an action for them at the common law."[9]

There must be some explanation other than expression of sentiment for the clear distinction made between first- and second-best things. Along with heirlooms Blackstone cites two other testamentary forms, *heriot* and *mortuary,* which "obtained pretty generally throughout most parts of the nation, and are therefore of more universal concern" (*Commentaries* 2:422–49). Both were a form of tithe. The latter one is of special interest to us as the origin of the phrase and concept of the "second best." The former, *heriot,* is associated with the notion of "the best."

After the 1600s, with the passing of power from the ecclesiastical courts, these customs simply did not come down to modern times and have been all but forgotten.

The bequest to his wife may express a similar religious concern, comparable to that of the tithe, in terms which had come to be just as formulaic as those with which the majority of medieval wills begin, except that the formula here is conveyed in the single phrase "second best." This formula, like the basic form of the will, can be traced to Anglo-Saxon origins.

These testamentary forms are of great significance to Shakespeare's will, but they are little known, having become obscured by time. To demonstrate their widespread use and ancient lineage, as well as their prominence in medieval and Renaissance life, and because they are so little known, I shall treat them at length.

HERIOTS: THE "BEST" THING

The ancient tithe known as *heriot* was of two sorts, heriot-*service* and heriot-*custom,* the former, according to Blackstone, amounting "to little more than a mere rent," while the latter "depended upon immemorial usage and custom" (*Commentaries* 422). Both were payable to the lord of the fee on the decease of the owner of the land. Blackstone traces the compulsory heriots to the Danes, finding in the laws of King Canute the several *hergeates* or heriots specified, which were exacted upon the death of a king's subject (*Commentaries* 423).

Most heriots were military in origin, consisting of arms, horses, and the "habiliments of war." Heriot was the equipment for war given by a lord to a retainer and returnable to the lord on the retainer's death. Doris M. Stenton found its military origin "still apparent in the eleventh century."[10] The military aspect is the only one recognized by Benjamin Thorpe in the glossary of *The Ancient Laws and Institutes of England:*

> *Here-geatu* for Here-geatwu (f.)—Relevatio, Relevium, Relief-heriot. The O. G. *heergewate,* "apparatus bellicus," military habiliments or equipments, which, after the death of the vassal, escheated to the sovereign or lord, to whom they were delivered by the heir.[11]

However, in the ensuing centuries, as this tithe continued to be observed, it lost its military significance and took on broader application as later definitions indicate. Of course, as the very title of one such source suggests, the tithe was not as widely practiced and therefore not as widely known as in former times. Heriots, or the variant *hariots,* were defined in the 1579 edition of John Rastell's *An Exposition of Certaine Difficult and Obscure Words, and Termes of the Lawes of This Realme . . . unto are also added the Old Tenures.* "Hariot service" is listed as "alwayes expressed in a man's grant, or deede that he holdeth by such service to pay hariot at the time of his death, and thys hariot is payable after the death of the tenant in fee simple"[12] (Fol. 136). To hold in fee simple, as Rastell defines it, is "to hold to any man or woman, to him and to his heires and to his assignes forevermore" (Fol. 201):

> Hariot custome, is where hariotes have bene payd tyme out of mynde by custome. And thys may be after the death of tenaunt for life &c but to speake thereof generally.

Rastell further identifies the kind and quality of thing long associated with this tithe:

> Hariot is the best beast (whether it bee Horse, Oxe, or Cow) that the tenaunt had at the tyme of hys death. And may bee eyther seysed, or a distresse taken for it, whether it bee hariot service, or hariot custome, to the Lordes use of whom the tenaunt held, by his Bailife or other officer belonging to his manour. (Fol. 136)

The heriot was the best live beast, or the best inanimate good, "but it is always a *personal* chattel," according to Blackstone. The vassal had to be the owner of it; and there could be no heriot on the death of a "feme-covert," for she can have no ownership in things personal (*Commentaries* 424).

The association of the heriot with the *best* thing was intrinsic to the word itself and to the distinction between this tithe and the other one related to it, that of the mortuary. We have it on the authority of Lord Chief Justice Sir Edward Coke that "in the Saxon tongue it is called Heregeat, as much to say, (as I take it) as the Lords best, for Here is Lord, and geat is best." And, he points out, "it hath beene anciently said, that the Herriot shall bee paid before the Mortuary" (*Coke on Littleton,* bk. 3, chap. 3, sec. 287, 185).

There is nothing designated as the "best" in Shakespeare's will. But then, by the seventeenth century, as we have seen, there was no legal reason for a heriot to be part of any will. The elder daughter and her husband are given the bulk of the estate, and specific items are simply denoted in terms of the person to whom the bequest was made. It is the very singularity of this residual formula in the will that so captured the attention of readers of the will. Since nothing else gives any indication that Shakespeare was concerned with the quality of the object, the attribution of "second best" becomes a kind of signal, made conspicuous by its singularity and by its having been an interlineation, added as it were, in the final draft of the document.

The mortuary to which Sir Edward Coke alludes in the quotation above is the type of tithe that sheds new light on Shakespeare's bequest to Anne.

MORTUARIES: THE SECOND BEST

With heriot, the mortuary or *sawolsceatt* (var. *sawelsceat, soulscot*), was, in the words of Dorothy Whitelock, a "characteristic feature" of the Anglo-Saxon will (*AS Wills* xli). It was customary to include this offering in the will, and according to Holdsworth it was "usually expressly left" (*Hist Eng Law* 3:545).

Using as his primary source the *Provinciale,* the collection of ecclesiastical laws by the foremost late-medieval English canonist, William Lyndwood (also spelled Lindewood), Blackstone defines mortuaries as a sort of ecclesiastical heriot, being claimed by and due to the minister in many parishes on the death of his parishioners. Originally they were only a voluntary bequest, "being intended, as Lyndwood informs us from a constitution of archbishop Langham, as a kind of expiation and amends to the clergy for the personal tithes, and other ecclesiastical duties, which the laity in their life-time might have neglected or forgotten to pay. For this purpose, after the Lord's heriot (or best good) was taken out, the second best chattel was reserved to the church as a mortuary: 'si decedens plura habuerit animalia, optimo cui de jure fuerit debitum reservato, ecclesiae suae sine dolo, fraude, seu contradictione qualibet, pro recompensatione subtractionis decimarum PERSONALIUM necnon et oblationum, secundum melius animal reservetur, post obitum, pro salute animae suae' (If they have several animals, the best of which should be reserved, the church may without injury, fraud or any contradiction whatsoever, for recompense, subtract from their personal tithe and offering, after death, according to the value of the animal reserved, for the good of their soul)."[13]

Heriots and mortuaries were so closely related that they were often interchanged by both editors and testators. C. W. Foster, the editor of *Lincoln Wills,* defines mortuaries as if they were heriots, presenting as usual practice the interchange that actually did not take place until later years when the law passed into custom:

> By a very ancient custom a gift or offering was due to the parish priest on the death of a parishioner. This gift was known as the ''soul-scot,'' ''principal,'' ''corse-present,'' or ''mortuary.'' Its nature and value were regulated by local custom, but it commonly consisted of the best horse, best beast, best garment, or other chattel: hence the name ''principal'' (Lat. *principalium*). It seems often to have been presented at the door of the church with the corpse [the laws called for it to be paid at the grave, as we have seen].

In the *Earliest English Wills* we also find instances where mortuary is treated of as the *principal:* that of John Olney, of Weston, 1420 (''and my beste best in the name off *principle*'' [47, 11. 18–19]) and that of Roger Flore (or Flower), Esq., 1424–25 (''And after my principal is taken, I wul my wyf haf my best ambeler, and my sone, sir Herre Plesyngton, wylk him likeþ best'' [57, 11. 34–35]). To bring the concept of Principal home to the modern reader, Furnivall furnishes the analogy of ''the survival of the Custom'' that ''may be seen at State funerals'' (n.4, 139).

As the customary observance of the heriot and the mortuary continued, such an interchange became more commonplace. The kinds of offerings came to be less strictly differentiated and rather freely interchanged:

> The heriot gives an occasion for what we may call a magisterial, though it is also a seignorial, intervention between the dead man and his heirs. Another such occasion is afforded by the soul-scot or mortuary. The dead man's parish church has a legal claim to a payment when he is buried. At least in later days, it generally claims the best, or the second best, beast or other chattel; very commonly the testator provides for his mortuary in his will. (322–23)

Citations given in the *Middle English Dictionary (MED)* and *A New English Dictionary on Historical Principles (NED)* will give the reader some idea of the span of centuries involved in the observance of this practice, from the late Middle Ages and into the 17th century following the time when Shakespeare's will was devised: "Prior . . . petivisset . . . versus Thomam le Forter, quandem partem bonorum que fuerunt Willi le Forter . . . defuncti . . . nomine Mortuarii, Ecclesie sue predicto debit, et per prefatum Thomam ei injuste detent" (*MED* 1330); "Or ellis þei schullen not be cristened, ne oyntid, ne biried wiþouten mortuarie" (*NED* 1380); "I will that the parson of Brympton have for me to his mortuarie a donne hors of mine" (*NED* 1469); "The parson and vicar wyll have for a mortuary . . . the best thygne that is about the house" (*NED* 1560); "they must have a mortuary, of every dead mans goods, and that was to be the *second best* [my italics] of the dead mans moveable goods or cattell" (*NED* 1647). The final date for the term's known use as a customary gift is 1897: "Mortuaries have been claimed by rectors and vicars within the memory of the present generation" (*NED*). The word came to apply to the ceremony itself: "Alle þo arn acursed þat for malyce forbydden oþere folk þat þey schulde noȝt offeryn at weddynges, at puryficacyouns, at mortuaryes, but o messe-peny (*MED* c. 1450); "Item: ij hangynges for a boue and beneth of blak bokrame for mortuaris" (*MED* 1466).[14]

With so much clear evidence of a long and widespread practice of this custom, why has it not been considered before in connection with the second best phrase in Shakespeare's will? I think C. W. Foster solves the riddle as to why this particular tithe has been overlooked for all these years when he explains in his editorial commentary to the *Lincoln Wills* that the phrase directing payment of mortuary has often been deleted from texts: "Almost every will in our period gives directions for the payment of a mortuary. These directions, when they consist of nothing more than such words as 'the mortuary that is due,' or 'my mortuary after the manner [*or* custom] of the town [*or* country *or* holy church]' have often been omitted in the printed abstract" (xxiii). A nineteenth-century editor had similarly "omitted some of the meaningless phrases," as E. A. J. Honigmann found in examining the will of Alexander Hoghton, Lancastrian and contemporary of Shakespeare, which, when restored to the text, proved to be of scholarly value.[15] The phrase may have appeared "meaningless" to modern editors, unfamiliar with the prominence given this offering in earlier times. An ancient legal directive noted in *Bouvier's Law Dictionary* cited by Blackstone in his *Commentaries* (II, 427) makes that prominence eminently clear: "a parishioner could not make a valid will without an assignment of a sufficient mortuary or gift to the church" (*Bouvier's Law Dictionary* 2264).

The force of this offering stemmed from its long history, not only because it was a basic aspect of ancient common law but perhaps even more because it was linked in its origins to ecclesiastical law. Ultimately it was transposed from the strictly ecclesiastical context to a wide-ranging social application as custom.

Essentially, there are two theories on the origin of the offering. Either it was derived from the pagan funeral practice of burying goods with the deceased and was then adopted for Christian use[16] or it originated from patristic sources. On this dispute between Germanic and patristic sources of the share of the soul, Sheehan shows that the teaching of the Fathers on the share of the soul was spread throughout northern Europe by Irish missionaries (292).[17] Sheehan observes that this rule of alms for the soul of the dead first appeared in the first code of Athelstan "among the church dues which the reeve was to enforce," although he acknowledges that the practice itself was much older. "One of the earliest wills of which a fairly complete report survives, mentions the grant of lands to the monastery at Deerhurst, the place of the donor's burial. Within the Empire, it was customary from the fourth century that Christians be allowed to choose their place of interment, and that some offering be made at the time of burial" (79).

In the laws of King Canute (1016–35) the mortuary is called soul-scot *(sawlsceat),* rendered in Latin as *symbolum animae,* or sometimes *sepultura* (*Commentaries* 425). The OED gives the etymology of *scat* as based in the Old Frisian *sket* and O.S. *skat,* meaning "treasure," and ON *skatt-r,* "tribute" and "treasure."

Soul-scot, after the OE *sawlsceat* or *sawul-(ge)sceot,* is defined by the OED as "a due paid on behalf of a deceased person to the Church of the parish to which he belonged; a mortuary."[18] For "Seelschatz," in *Die Gesetze der Angelsachsen* (2:647),[19] Liebermann presents several distinct points. Soul-scot developed from the death division of one-third of the movable goods which was given at the grave for the benefit of the soul *(zugunsten der Seele);* Innocent IV explains that the custom in England was one-third of the goods. It was "under eternal threat" that soulscot was paid to the parish to which the dead one belonged. Soul-scot is paid at the edge of the still-open grave as the first guilt offering for the one struck down. It was for those who died unabsolved, without confession, for being unabsolved was considered as a sinful lack of care for one's own soul. The size or amount of the gift to the parish to which one belonged was according to one's means. In the thirteenth century the church forbade communal potations for the good of the soul; the pastor, or parish priest, is obligated "to repay in a heartfelt way" the soulscots through masses, singing of psalms, and alms. Finally, the vassal was to his unconditional lord mostly obligated for the soul, that is, for the pious gifts.

The religious aspect was emphasized by Joseph Bosworth in *The Anglo-Saxon Dictionary,* where he defines *sawel-sceatt* as "an ecclesiastical due, to be paid for every deceased person to the clergy of the church to which he belonged, in consideration of the services performed by them in his behalf."[20] As Bosworth further claims, "It appears to have been one of the objects of the early gilds, to provide for the payment of this fee." According to Liebermann, the guild to which one belonged gave to the church for the soul of its brother buttered slices of bread *("geschmierte Brote")* (2:647).

The value of the *scot* in England from c. 590 to 780 has been assessed by Liebermann in *Die Gesetze der Angelsachsen* as having been comparable to a penny (2:634). He records a usage of *scot* in connection with guilt, or debt, in an old formula spoken by one who denies being guilty of owing money: "I am guilty to you neither of scot nor coin, neither penny nor penny's worth" ("ich schulde dir nicht sceatt noch Schilling, nicht Pfennig noch Pfennigswert"). The Elizabethan source we have referred to before, Rastell's dictionary on obscure terms, includes *scot* and shows how by 1579 (and extending to the 1609 edition) it had come to general usage, losing its ecclesiastical significance: "Scot, that is to bee quite of a certen custome, as of common tallage made to the use of the Sherife or his Bailifes" (Fol. 180). Through her work on early wills Whitelock found evidence that "in Anglo-Saxon times the *Sawolsceatt* was a third of the goods, and it is sometimes paid in land" (*AS Wills* 109–10).

The obligatory nature of the tithe is also clear from its earlier appearance in the laws. The ordinance of King Edgar indicates that soul-scot had come to be accepted as "due on behalf of every Christian man" (*AS Charters* 23). The first mention is in Athelstan's ordinance on church dues, c. 930 (Whitelock, *Councils and Synods* 46): "Though an ancient due, this is not mentioned before this in the laws, but it occurs in 899 in a lease of Bishop Werferth" (46).

It was not always referred to as soul-scot, as we learn from Blackstone, who found in Selden's *History of Tithes* that this fee was also referred to as a "corse-present" since "anciently it was brought to church with the corpse," or as cited in the *Lincoln Wills,* "presented at the door of the church with the corpse."[21]

Whitelock includes in *Councils and Synods* both a law of King Æthelred in which *saulsceat* is specified as payment for the soul which is always paid at the open grave (352) and also an ecclesiastical code in which again it is specified that *sawlsceat* is always paid at the open grave (393). In the ordinance of Æthelred as well as the law of Canute the rite is explicitly ordained as the following citations (and translations) by Whitelock clearly show:

> Æthelred:
> And sawlscat is rihtast þæt man
> symle gelæste æt openum græfe.
> [And it is best that payment for the
> souls of the dead should always be
> rendered before the grave is closed.] (*AS Charters* 82–83)
> Canute:
> And sawlsceat is rihtast þæt man symle
> gelæste á æt openum græfe.
> [And it is best that payment for the
> souls of the dead should always be
> rendered before the grave is closed.] (167)

Whitelock observes of Wynflaed's will that the term *saulsceatte* is used generally for "any charitable payments for the good of her soul," but that it is often used "in a more limited sense," as "a payment to the religious foundation as a price for burial." This due, for which the Latin equivalent is *sepultura,* was not a voluntary payment, as Professor Whitelock points out, and had to be paid "to the mynster which has the right to it, even if the body is buried elsewhere" (*AS Wills* 109–10).

The custom varied from place to place, not only as to the mortuary to be paid but also as to the person to whom it was payable. In the archdeaconry of Chester it was the custom that the bishop should have "at the death of every clergymen dying therin, his best horse or mare, bridge, saddle, and spurs, his best gown or cloak, hat, upper garment under his gown, and tippet and also his best signet or ring" (Sheehan 79).

The usual form of the will deals with this tithe first as we see from a sample presented in *A Concise History of Common Law* by T. F. T. Plucknett: first comes the bequeathing of the soul to God and the saints and of the body to a particular church. Then come funeral arrangements. Then "in many places custom requires the bequest of the best beast as a mortuary (the mediaeval ghost was frequently seen astride the mortuary which was a heavy charge upon small estates). . . . If the lord took the best beast as heriot, the parson would have to be content with the second best as mortuary.''[22]

The procedure is thus summarized in Pollock and Maitland:

> His soul he bequeath to God, the Virgin and the saints; his body to a certain church. Along with his body he gives his mortuary, or his *principal* (principale), or corspresent; one of the best chattels that he has; often, if he is a knight, it will be his warhorse. Both Glanvill and Bracton have protested that neither heriot nor corspresent is demanded by general law, though custom may exact it.[23]

Blackstone confirmed that ''in Judge Bracton's time, so early as Henry III, it was riveted into an established custom: insomuch that the bequests of heriots and mortuaries were held to be necessary ingredients in every testament of chattels: 'Imprimis autem debet quilibet, qui testamentum fecerit, dominum suum de meliori re quam habuerit recognoscere; et postea ecclesiam de alia meliori' (the lord must have the best good left him as an heriot; and the church the second best as a mortuary)'' (*Commentaries* 426). By the eleventh century soul-scot had come to cover all the property, whether land or chattels, which a testator devoted to religious purposes.

The epithet ''second best'' is derived from a traditional formula for the mortuary, such as that which we find in Blackstone's *Commentaries:* ''[A]fter the lord's heriot or best good was taken out, the second best chattel was reserved to the church as a mortuary'' (425). It was the next best thing (*OED:* 1 ''Next in quality to the first,'' and Shakespeare's bequest to Anne is the example given), and it was directly related to the particular meaning of reparation for his soul.

Historically, the phrase took on significances derived from two longstanding aspects of the law governing mortuaries, gradually becoming part of a custom that signified both aspects we have seen attributed to it in its early usage, namely, reparation and reconciliation. As William Easterby explained in 1888, in *The History of the Law of Tithes in England,*[24] mortuaries could be likened to ''Conscience-money,'' which in his day was ''received by the Chancellor of the Exchequer.'' Such ideas were an inextricable part of this offering. The following pages will illustrate to what extent the ''second best'' bed was meant as an ''offering'' (or something like that).

THE SECOND BEST BED AS TITHE OF REPARATION

Mortuary or *sawol-sceat,* along with plow alms and *cyric-sceat,* was one of the major sources of ecclesiastical revenue. F. M. Stenton proposed in *Anglo-Saxon England* that these were in essence the first forms of tithes. Plow alms consisted of a penny paid within a fortnight after Easter for each plow team working in a parish.[25] *Cyric-sceat* or "church-scot," according to Stubbs, was "a sort of commutation for first fruits paid by every householder" in addition to his tithe. Until the late sixteenth century *cyric-sceat* followed the law as set by Ine: it had to be paid at Martinmas (November 11), "according to the hearth that a man is at at midwinter, that is in the township where he keeps Christmas."[26]

The religious nature of these tithes is underscored by the dates assigned to the payment of each one. The days of observance were legally established and, being tied in with liturgical observance, were a part of the very grain of social life. The specific days of payment were ordained by law, as we find clearly set out in the following law included in John Mitchell Kemble's thorough study *The Saxons in England:*

> And let God's dues be willingly paid every year; that is, plough-alms fifteen days after Easter, the tithe of young by Pentecost, and of the fruits of the earth by Allhallows' Mass, and Rome-fee by St. Peter's mass, and lightshot thrice a year. (Kemble 547)

Benjamin Thorpe, in *The Ancient Laws and Institutes of England,* cites the tithes and days due as they were specified in the canons enacted under King Edgar: "plough-alms, xv days after Easter; and a tithe of young, by Pentecost; and of earth-fruits, by All Saints; and 'Rom-feoh' [Peter's pence], by St. Peter's mass; and church-scot, by Martinmas."[27] Kemble includes a similar portion from Æthelred's law in *The Saxons in England,* where *cyricsceat* is defined as "first fruits of seed" in "The Income of the Clergy" (appendix B).[28]

Sawl sceat was "a present made to a church where the testator desired to rest, in consideration of religious services to be performed for the good of his soul" (468, 490). And apparently there was yet another fee due, namely lightshot ("leoht-gesceot" in the *Anglo-Saxon Dictionary*): "a contribution made to furnish the church with lights" (633).

Before the seventh century, such ecclesiastic dues had by custom been divided into four parts—one for the bishop, one for the poor, one for the clergy, and one for the repairs of the fabric. But as we learn from

Kemble, "In his rules for the government of the newly-planted English church, Gregory directed Augustine to make three instead of four portions, since he as a monk could have no separate share of his own" (479).

Stiff penalties for nonpayment of ecclesiastic dues were imposed as the laws indicate:

> Cyricsceat: 'Be cyricsceattum. Cyricsceattas sýn ágifene be Seint Martines maessan. Gif hwa ðæt he gelaéste, sý he scyldig LX scill. and be twelffealdum ágyfe ðone cyricsceat. And ic wille eác ðæt mine geréfan gedón ðaet man agyfe ða cyricsceattas and ða sawl-sceattas to ðam stowum, ðe hit mid rihte tó gebyrige. (Appendix D, 559)
> [Concerning churchshot. Churchshot is to be rendered by Saint Martin's Mass [Martinmas]. Anyone who has not carried out payment by this day is liable for 60 shillings and required to render it twelvefold. And each was to carry this out by giving the churchshot and the soul-scot to that place to which by right he belonged.]

Thus, the obligation to pay the fees was ever being reiterated—and in a variety of contexts. In an eleventh-century "Pastoral Letter," Wulfstan, Bishop of Worcester and Archbishop of York, exhorted the thanes, both clerical and lay, to heed their yearly dues so as to die free of indebtedness: "ðaet is sulhælmessan [plow alms] romenegas [Peter's pence] cyricsceattas [church shot] & leohtgescota [light dues]."[29]

The main point here, and the one of the utmost importance with regard to Shakespeare's will, is the traditionally recognized connection between soul-scot and restitution. As F. M. Stenton points out, accruing to the familiar significance of the mortuary fee, or soul-scot, there was another, equally familiar meaning—it "was often rationalized as a payment for neglected tithes" (153).

This meaning of the mortuary is evident by the second half of the thirteenth century when mortuary served as restitution to the parish church for failure to pay tithes or other dues. Sir Edward Coke cites a ruling in "On Restitutions" called the "secundum quid," in which the heir is ordered to make restitution "in blood only, (that is to make his retort as heir in blood to the party attainted and other his ancestors, and not to any dignity, inheritance of lands, etc.) and this is a restitution *secundum quid,* or in part" (*Coke on Littleton* 240). Thus, preoccupation with the repair of injustice, typical of the wills of the period, is evident in this point of law as well. The constitution of Simon Langham (1366–

68) ruled that "the second-best beast of every parishioner who possessed three animals was to be paid, as recompense for personal tithes which parishioners had by oversight omitted to pay."[30] The term in this sense was included in Cowell's *The Interpreter; or, Booke Containing the Signification of Words,* even as late as 1708: "Mortuary, *(mortuarium, mortarium,)* Is a gift left by a man at his death to his parish church, for the recompence of his personal tithes and offerings not duly paid in his life-time . . . the best to the lord for a heriot, the second for a mortuary."

The penitential aspect of the mortuary is evident even in its origins, which I believe may be traced farther back in church history than is allowed by some scholars who argue that tithes were late additions to the church. John Godfrey claims that the four-fold division of revenues such as I have been discussing came to be replaced by the system of tithes, tithe "not as old as Christianity itself," since it is "not mentioned in the canons of the great councils from Nicaea to Chalcedon."[31]

However, church history seems more ably served by Kemble, who traces the antiquity of the custom of tithes to the ancient Poenitentials and Confessionals, citing an eighth-century work by Theodor intended for the instruction of the clergy:

> Tributum aecclesiae sit, sicut est consuetudo provinciae, id est, ne tantum pauperes in decimis, aut in aliquibus rebus vim patiantur. Decimas non est legitimum dare, nisi pauperibus et peregrinis.[32]
> [Let the Ecclesiastical tithing be according to the custom of the Province, that is, not only must everyone render the tithe in money, but also in other possessions as well. It is not legitimate to exclude the tithe, even for the poor or strangers.]

The anonymous collection *Tithes and Oblations, according to the Laws Established by the Church of England* (1595) also held tithing to have been established "by divine constitution," tracing it to Moses "by whom it was delivered (at the appointment of God)." And Blackstone in the *Commentaries* attributes the establishment of tithes in English municipal law as having been "probably in imitation of the Jewish law" (II, ch. 3, 25). The first law he found in a constitutional decree was that in a synod held in A.D. 786.

Any tracing of the origins of these customs should ultimately consider the Jewish sacrificial offerings defined in Leviticus. All offerings were presented at the door of the Tabernacle in the Temple, where they were given over to the priests for various rituals of distribution or burning upon the altar. There were four sacrificial offerings: the burnt offering of bullocks, rams, goats, doves and pigeons; the meal offerings of grain, etc., without leaven; peace offerings of cattle, sheep or goats; and sin offerings and trespass offerings (both sacrifices of reparation), the offerings differing according to the nature of the sins. Whenever the rights of God or of neighbor had been violated, a sacrifice of reparation had to be made.

In the Genevan Bible, the translation popular in Reformation Churches of England and undoubtedly known to Shakespeare,[33] in Leviticus 5: 9–10, the sin offering is two turtle doves or two young pigeons, the first for a sin offering and the second as a burnt offering "as the maner is" [Marginal note c: "Or, according to the lawe"] "ſo ſhal the Prieſt make an atonement for him (for his inne which he hathe committed) and itſhalbe forgiuen him" (47). A "treſ paſſe offring" was for transgression "As touching the firſt ſrutes or tithes, due to the Prieſt's and Leuites; and consisted of "a Ram without blemiſh." The distinction between "best" and "second-best" may be explicitly stipulated, or it may be implicit as when the specification "without blemish" is given for the offerings.[34]

According to Reginald R. Sharpe, in *The Calendar of Wills, Proven and Enrolled in the Court of Husting, London, A.D. 1258–A.D. 1688,* the mortuary was considered "of greater interest than the heriot, for it was demanded from a larger portion of the population, being a spiritual reparation, and although minimal offerings were established by custom, testators very often exercised some freedom of choice in its regard." The most common offering of freemen and peasants was a horse, or ox or other animals placed before the body of the deceased in the funeral procession; the terms *principale* and *corse-present* (and sometimes "foredrove" from the custom of driving animals at the head of the funeral procession) express both the quality of the offering and the occasion when it was made (*Calendar of Wills* vii).

Thus, historically, the mortuary was a kind of reparation for failure to pay that which was due by a sort of legalized spiritual bond. The mortuary was still widely practiced in the sixteenth century as the examples in *Lincoln Wills* exhibit. They also demonstrate the kinds of excesses into which mortuary had fallen and indicate the way in which heriot and mortuary were merging into custom. Instead of the second best, the best is most frequently the deposition in later years, i.e., the "heriot" had become intermixed with the mortuary fee. The mortuary gift in these wills appears as the "best beast" or "the best quick good" thirty-three times; the best horse, three times; the best cow once; the best garments, the best instrument, three times; and the best thing or best good, twenty-three times (xxiii). The lord of the manor's portion has been subsumed by the authority of the court. Two of the wills attest the concerns for the good of the soul or for restitution of "oblacions and tithes forgottyn." Similarly:

The Testament of Thomas Rawsby, of Harmston, 1505: "Also I bequeath in the name of my mortuary my best beast." (2:2)

The Testament of John Cod, of Hemswell, 1522: "I bequethe my best beist accordingly to the lawe and custome for my mortuary." (10)

The Testament of Joan Raynton, of Middle Rasen Tupholme, 1523: "I will have iiij trentalles to be done for my husband soule and my soulc and it may be bourne of my goodes." (11)

The Testament of Richard Symonde, of Hackthorn, 1523: "I bequeth in the name of my mortuary my best beast. To the high altar of hackthron for forgotten tithes iiijd. (11)

The Testament of Robert Staveley, of Gainsborough, 1523: "I bequeth in the name of my mortuary my best goode affter the maner off the cuntre." (11)

The Testament of John Leek of Boston, Mercer, [1520–31]: "I will that Jenet my wyff have the parler that I ly in the space off a yere affter my deth; . . . I will the sayd Jenet have the bed that stondyth in the parlor, with iiij pillowys, j off the best and iij off the next best, and all thynges that longyth therto, hallf a garnysh of vessyll, halff a dosen sylver sponys, a sylver salte parcell gilte, with the cover off the same, and my musterdevillys gowne." (41)

The Testament of Christopher Yonge of Brant Boughton, 1529: "Also my best best to be my mortuary." (123)

Even as late as 1642 the phrases appear in wills, as in the case of "one John Shakespere of Budbrook, near Warwick," who left his father-in-law his "best boots" (H-P, *Outlines* 258).

That it was still an accepted fact of death even as late as the early seventeenth century may be seen from *A Briefe Treatise of Testaments and Last Willes* by Henry Swinburne to which I have referred considerably for information on civil testamentary law. In the 1611 edition, he duly records the statutes concerning mortuaries, following the ordinance set out in 21 Hen.8, ch.6. In this statute precise fees were fixed to correct the abuses that had come to abound, more than one mortuary often being exacted, for instance. The impact made by the law on the custom is recorded in the *Lincoln Wills:*

> *The Testament* of Hugh Schawe, 15[30–31]: ''with my mortuary aftyr the acte of parliament late mayd, and the custom of the towne of Boston. I bequethe, for myn oblacions and tithes forgottyn, to the holy sacrament iiijs, iiijd.'' (190).

According to the 1542 edition of *The principall lawes and statutes of Englande,* no one should be compelled to pay for a mortuary more than was due:

> No persone spirituall theyr fermers nor bayliffes shal cal any person before any iudge spiritual for the recovery of any Mortuaries more then is hereafter mencioned upon payne to forfait for every time so much in value as they shal take above ye sume here limitted & over that xl š to ye prie greved, for which he shal have an action of det by wiyt byl or informatiõ[n], wherein no wager of law essoin nor petitiõ[n], shalbe alowed. First no mortuarie shalbe taken of any whych at hys death hath in movable goodes under the value of x marke. Also no Mortuarye shall be taken but only where Mortuaries have bene used to be payde, and there after the forme herafter mencioned. Nor in no mo places but one, that is to wete, there where hys most abyding in and there but one. Nor no persone shal take for a Mortuarye of any person beyng at hys death of the value of x markes above his dettes paid & under xxx.li above š. iiv & And of ye value of xxx.li and under lx., not above vi.š viii. . . .
>
> Nevertheles such spiritual person may take anythynge whiche shalbe disposed or bequethed to hym or to the hyghe aulter of the church. Also nothynge shalbe taken for Mortuarie in Wales nor in ye marches of the same. . . .
>
> No woman was to pay nor any child, nor anyone of full age that is not a house keeper, nor any wayfaring man; but such wayfaring man's mortuary shall be paid in the parish to which he belongs.[35]

Swinburne's prohibitions on mortuaries in certain counties of Wales are further indication that the observance continued ''where Mortuaries have been accustomed to bee taken'' (272^{v} / Nn4^{v}–273 / Nn5).

Of course, it may strike us as peculiar that while this very law was set up to remedy abuses, the king as titular ecclesiastical head meanwhile became the recipient of both ecclesiastical tithes and court taxes, making for a situation fraught with abuses of other kinds. But the main point is that ecclesiastical law was for centuries reinforced by civil law in this matter of church dues. It was a tradition imbedded in both legal systems, and even in this very statute, which marks the beginning of the end of its practice, it retains its essential substance: it was expected to be paid upon death, and it was to be paid in only one place, the place of the deceased's "most abyding in."

Oversight in matters of mortuaries continued under diocesan authority. As Christopher Kitching points out, "As diocesans they [the bishops] were attempting to preserve as much of the deceased's property as possible from diminution by excessive fees and costs of probate, and thus to ensure sufficient remainder to fulfill the obligations of the deceased to his family and to promote charitable benefactions for the good of his soul" (Heal and O'Day 194).

What we must keep in mind regarding Shakespeare's will is that, as an offering to be paid to the place of most abiding, its significance was retained as a tithe of reconciliation, and as such it was retained even when the law of soul-scot was changed in other regards. This reconciliation aspect could explain why the phrase "second best" eventually appears in connection with so many different kinds of items as bequests in medieval and Renaissance wills. Indeed, as I will show in the following chapter, it is likely that Shakespeare himself was most singularly informed of the ancient laws that demonstrate the significance of the reconciliation aspect of mortuary law.

Soul-scot usually went to the priest, but in the early days, according to Margaret Deanesly in *The Pre-Conquest Church in England: An Ecclesiastical History of England,* "the thegn who built the church sometimes claimed to take these offerings, or the greater part of them." The code known as II Edgar, apparently published at Andover before 962, is of great importance, "for its direction as to the recipients of tithe and church dues: . . . And soul's scot shall be paid for each Christian man to the minster that gives him burial (this would apply to any church with a graveyard)."[36]

Several Anglo-Saxon leases and grants of land make the payment of soul-scot the condition of fulfilling the legal requirements for acquisition, such as the lease by Ealhferth, Bishop of Winchester: "leased 8 hides of land at Easton for three lives to their dear friend Earl Cuthred and to Wulfthryth, his wife, and to one man of his own choice in addition, to hold and enjoy . . . free from every burden except the construction of bridges and military service and the payment of eightfold church dues *[ciricsceattan]* and priests' dues *[measseprestas gereohta]* and burial fees *[saulsceattas]*." Similarly, King Eadred granted to "thegn" Alfsige Hunlafing an estate of five hides at Alwalton, "free of every burden except the building of bridges and military service; a prudent landowner [will also make himself responsible for] church dues, burial fees and tithes *[Ciric-sceat, saulsceat teogeðunga]''* (*AS Charters,* 26–27 and 56–57; on the legal enforcement of *saul sceattas,* see I Aethelstan 4 and later codes).

The payments were made to the church of the parish to which the deceased person belonged, even if he was buried elsewhere (see V Æthelred, 12, 1 and later codes). The Laws of Ine, recorded in the *English Historical Documents,* read: ''Church-scot is to be paid from the haulm and the hearth where one resides at midwinter'' (Liebermann: *ciricsceat* mon sceal agifan to þam healme 7 to þam heorðe, þe se mon on bið to middum wintra [2:116]). With regard to the term ''midwinter'' Dorothy Whitelock, the editor, notes that it ''usually means Christmas, but as church-scot was due at Martinmas (11 November)'' (n. 2, 406). Edgar's code followed Ine's in specifying that the payment for the soul was to be paid for every Christian man to the minster to which it belongs, ''to be rendered by Martinmas under pain of the full fine, which the law-book prescribes'' (*Eng Hist Doc* 405 and 431–32).[37] In Liebermann the code reads: ''7 laeste man saulsceat æt ælcan Cristenan men to þam mynstre, þe hit togebyrige'' (2:200) (''And every Christian man shall render payment for the soul to that minster to which he belonged.'') In Æthelred, according to Liebermann, we find ''7 saulsceat is rihtast, þæt man symle gelæste æt openum græfe. 7 gyf man aenig lic of rihtscriftscire elles hwar lecge, gelæste man saulsceat swa þeh into þam mynstre, þe hit to hyrde'' (2:240; see also 2:294) (''And it is best that payment for the soul of the dead always be rendered at the open grave. And even if a man's body is buried elsewhere than in his rightful parish, he shall render payment for the soul to the minster to which he belongs as an obligation'').

Æthelred's code of 1008 calls for payment even ''if any body is buried elsewhere, outside the proper parish; the payment for the soul is nevertheless to be paid to the minster to which it belonged.'' Æthelred underscores his fervor: ''And all God's dues are to be furthered zealously, as is needful'' (*Eng Hist Doc* 444). In the Old English will of Aelfric, Archbishop of Canterbury (1002–5), mention is made of ''burial fee,'' which is the translation made of what Dorothy Whitelock notes as ''literally, 'soul-payment' '' (he gave his best ship to his lord) (*Eng Hist Doc* 589).

LAW AND CUSTOM

Law and custom may become inextricably bound, as I believe was the case with mortuary over the centuries of its practice among the people. As Edward Jenks observes of custom in relation to law, ''It lives in the consciousness of the community'' (*SEAALH* 1:163). Somehow in the consciousness of generations there seems to have developed a special significance for the ''second best'' of a thing. It was something like a ritual word, as may be seen in its early usage in Jewish tithing law.

ECCLESIASTICAL LAW SUBSUMED BY CIVIL LAW

Shakespeare's will does not stipulate a payment for his soul, but he does include a commendation of his soul to the hands of his Creator. The absence of any direct statement shows the extent to which the law as law had lost effect in the Reformation while still retaining its hold upon the popular mind as custom. As Schoenbaum expresses it regarding the custom of dower law, ''Custom functions when the wills are silent'' (*Comp Doc Life* 301). I believe the ''second best'' type of bequest exemplifies the same development: with the secularization of English law, what had once been observed as a sacred, solemn decree under canon law now lost its legal force but retained its hold among the people as a custom associated with reparation and reconciliation.

The formula ''second best'' could communicate all or most of the significances covered thus far, namely: an acknowledgment of dues in consideration of services done in behalf of the testator; a kind of reparation for tithes and dues neglected or not duly paid in the testator's lifetime; or an act of reconciliation in terms of payment to the ''minster'' to which the testator belonged, dwelled in, or lived the most. The formula operated somewhat like a genre of testamentary expression conveying in its form a given content.

As Eber Carle Perrow points out in his study ''The Last Will and Testament as a Form of Literature,'' ''The use of the metaphor in making bequests became a marked feature of medieval wills.'' This feature assumes two forms: ''willing of tangible property with metaphorical significance . . . or it may be intangible things such as love, hate, diseases, and the like that are bequeathed. Sometimes the metaphor is applied to only one or two of the bequests, and at other times it is carried throughout the testament so consistently as to approach allegory'' (709). The ''metaphorical bequest may have arisen largely from the suggestions offered by the New Testament, which . . . was considered as the Last Will of Jesus'' (709).

It is significant that though the phrase appears in many other wills of the period, ''second best bed'' is the only instance of its use in this particular will. No other real property is designated as either best or second best. Perhaps we today confuse the phrase ''second best'' with the one more in current use, ''second-class.'' Could the emphasis not be read as on the aspect of ''best''? A thing is not best, but *is* second *best?* We may surely accept the fact that for most of those living in Elizabethan England the concept of the ''second best'' was traditional and not unfamiliar.

Given the various kinds of items designated in the wills and laws we have examined, it is possible that the item itself was intended as an indication, token, or symbol of the matter about which the testator wished to make amends. Based on such an assumption, the choice of a bed as a legacy leaves little doubt as to the area of concern, but what it was meant to convey about the concern has been the subject of controversy.

We may, if we are given to such speculation, take Shakespeare's use of the phrase ''second best'' in conjunction with a bed as confession that he has been negligent in fulfilling those offices Anne had every right to require of him and is offering her the usual formulaic reparation. In the juxtaposition of the bed and second best, rather than intending, as interpretations have made of it, either to disparage their conjugal life as having been ''second best,'' with the implication that another relationship has been ''best,'' or to leave his wife only an actual bed of second best value, Shakespeare could have had in mind any or all of the meanings associated with the phrase. He could have been acknowledging services she has done on his behalf; indicating reparation for dues neglected or not duly paid in his life-time; or even expressing a desire for reconciliation as a final act of his life. I do not think we could go so far as to say that the phrase itself is an expression of warmth or tenderness; however, as a metaphor, it is undeniably poignant in all the meanings clustered within it, especially in its exclusive application to the circumstances of one's last days. Though we cannot say with certainty that these are the intended meanings, Shakespeare's probable knowledge of mortuary law makes it difficult to think that the choice of this particular phrase was anything but deliberate.

Another indication that he had the ancient mortuary meanings in mind may be the placement of the interlineation. As our examination of medieval and Renaissance laws and wills has shown, the best bed by

Shakespeare's time was usually left to the elder son, there being no longer a feudal lord to receive the disposition of heriot. Moreover, as we have seen, Shakespeare's will satisfies all the requirements of the ancient law by which, in the event a man has no son, the eldest daughter receives the chief messuage. The legacy to Anne is interlineated after the long bequest to his elder daughter, Susanna, an appropriate placement in terms of coming after the disposition of all other property (including what one can safely assume is the "best" bed) to the elder child.

But the most significant thing about the placement is that it comes at the end of nineteen lines devoted to the "yssueinge" of "the Right heires of me the saied William Shackspere for ever." The insertion of his "wief" and his "bed" here is a gesture of great importance, stressing the magnitude of their marriage bond through succeeding generations to come. In addition, the bequest is placed between the surviving children, so to speak, coming as it does after the one to Susanna and before the heirloom bequest to Judith, lending further weight to the interpretation that argues against a slur upon their relationship.

His choice of the phrase may also be taken as an expression to Anne of their shared provincial and fundamentally medieval (perhaps even religious) backgrounds. The phrase had been in common use for centuries and always in the most profoundly sacred context. Hence, it could have expressed not only something about the bond between them but the common bonds of custom and mortality as well.

But whatever one may choose to believe about Shakespeare's intent in using the formula, no one can now deny the manifold meanings and associations, or his knowledge of them, which have been lost through the intervening centuries to our own time.

When the will is considered within the context of family history in the years leading up to the poet's death, surely the question of its intent can be settled.

Chapter Five

The Will as Family Testament

> "Put thine house in order, for thou shalt die and not live," 2 Kings 20.
> Epigraph to Swinburne, *Brief Treatise*

The personal nuances in Shakespeare's will become more evident against the backdrop of crucial events involving his immediate family and friends during the last twenty years of his life. From 1596, the year of the first personal crisis, until 1616, when he died, family matters were at the forefront in both his personal life and the plots of plays produced in corresponding years.

In August 1596, Shakespeare's only son, Hamnet (Judith's twin), died. Two months later, in October, heraldic arms for John Shakespeare, the poet's father, were granted. The following year, 1597, finds Shakespeare taking the major step toward Stratford residency in the purchase of New Place, the second largest house in Stratford, buying it from William Underhill, Jr. (whose father was an Inner Temple lawyer). The poet probably settled his family there the same year. It was from that same time his sister and brother-in-law lived at the Henley Street house, his birthplace. Schoenbaum places his settling into New Place at the end of 1597 or the beginning of 1598 (*Doc Life* 178). By 1598, he wanted to buy forty acres of land in Shottery, Anne's birthplace, where the dwelling known as "Anne Hathaway's cottage" is now located. Thus, he was clearly expanding his holdings in Stratford, a development which may be viewed as a reflection of his re-establishing (or reclaiming) of family ties as well, even though he must have divided his residence between Stratford and London since his personal testimony in the Belott-Mountjoy case is that he lived at the Mountjoy's in London from 1598 to 1604 and had known the family for thirteen years, though there is no evidence as to how long he continued to live there after 1604.[1]

The exact date of his retirement to Stratford is not known, but the second in a series of family crises that might have brought him back was his father's death and burial, on September 8, 1601. Upon his father's death he succeeded to the two houses in Henley Street, a cottage across Chapel Lane from the garden of New Place (Bentley 43). On May 1, 1602, he purchased property in Old Stratford, 107 acres (for the sum of £320) from William Combe, a lawyer of Middle Temple, and his nephew John. Indeed, in addition to becoming more involved with his own family, Shakespeare appears to have become concerned in the Combe family as well, as references to Shakespeare after his return to Stratford ''more often relate him to the Combes than to any other local family'' (EKC 2:127 ff.). In a will dated January, 1613, he received a legacy of £5 from John Combe, who died in 1614. In relation to this family, the reader may recall that it was to Thomas Combe, Jr., that Shakespeare bequeathed his sword. Thomas, Jr., was only seven years old at the time of the probate of Shakespeare's will, old enough possibly to have been a friend of Elizabeth Hall, the poet's granddaughter, who was close to the same age.

As of 1603, he must still have been acting in London, for his name is registered as one of the original actors in Ben Jonson's *Sejanus* at the Globe that year. ''This Tragoedie was first acted, in the yeere 1603. By the King's Majesties Servants. The principall Tragoedians were Ric. Burbage, Aug. Philips, Will. Sly, John. Lowin, Will. Shake-speare, Joh. Hemings, Hen. Condel, Alex. Cooke'' (Gray 162). On May 17, 1603, there is a record of King James issuing a patent establishing Shakespeare's company as His Majesty's Players. Yet, according to the Fines of the Court of King's Bench, sometime that year (possibly as a result of a bad outbreak of the plague that year?), Shakespeare purchased a messuage at Stratford, with barns, gardens, and orchards, for a sum of £60 from Hercules Underhill.[2]

His personal involvement in family and local affairs shows up the next year when in 1604 he sued Philip Rogers, an apothecary, for the sum of 30 shillings and 10 pence, the balance of an account for malt and a small loan of money (Gray 163). On July 24, 1605, he bought for £440 from Ralph Huband ''the unexpired term of thirty-one years of a moiety of the great and small tithes of Stratford, Old Stratford, Bishopton and Welcombe'' (Gray 163). According to Gerald Eades Bentley, *Shakespeare: A Biographical Handbook,* this was ''the largest investment which is known to us,'' and which ''derives from a complicated historical situation arising out of the dissolution of the monasteries a generation before Shakespeare was born.''[3] When monasteries were abolished in the reign of Henry VIII, the vast land holdings for which the tenants paid rents or tithes had to be transferred. In 1553, when Stratford was incorporated, many of these tithes were turned over to the town corporation. In turn the Corporation made long-term leases to various individuals who either paid an annual fee to the town or subleased to others. It was one of the subleases Shakespeare bought (44).

The renewed personal involvement may be accepted as confirmed from a record of sale of July 1605, where he is described as being ''of Stratford-upon-Avon, Gentleman.'' Since he was similarly designated three years earlier, in 1602, when hc was apparently still in London, Halliwell-Phillipps concludes that ''after the acquisition of New Place, he had taken up a permanent abode in his native town'' (H-P, *Life* 172).

Shakespeare's family life took on another dimension when two years later he became an in-law for the first time—on June 5, 1607, Susanna married John Hall, she being twenty-five, he thirty-two. Susanna and her husband lived only a short distance from New Place. Shakespeare thought highly enough of his son-in-law, only eleven years younger than the poet (Eccles 111), to name him—along with Susanna—executor of his will. John Hall was a doctor and a very devout Protestant. In the English edition he prepared of his Latin casebook he gives thanks many times to God for the successful cure of his patients. Apparently, as a prayer he wrote indicates, he believed himself to have had a miraculous recovery: ''Thou hast saved me . . . restoring me as it were from the very jaws of death to former health, for which I praise Thy Name, O most mercifull God, and Father of our Lord Jesus Christ, praying thee to give me a most thankful heart for this great favour, for which I have cause to admire thee.'' He showed his gratitude by giving Holy Trinity Church a carved pulpit and by serving as church warden for the year 1628–29 (*Doc Life* 236). He was buried in 1635 beside his wife in the row of five Shakespeare family graves inside the chancel of Trinity Church. The strong identification of Shakespeare's family members is apparent from John Hall's gravestone, where Susanna is listed as ''the daughter and coheire of William Shakespeare, Gent.'' (Bentley 47), and also in the epitaph engraved on Susanna's gravestone:

> Witty above her sexe, but that's not all,
> Wise to salvation was good Mistris Hall;

Something of Shakspere was in that, but this
Wholy of Him with whom she's now in blisse.
Then, Passenger, ha'st ne'er a teare
To weepe with her that wept with all;—
That wept, yet set her selfe to chere
Them up with comforts cordiall?
Her love shall live, her mercy spread,
When thou ha'st nere a teare to shed.
(H-P, *Outlines* 277)

The Halls moved into New Place when Shakespeare died and remained there for the remainder of their lives (*Doc Life* 237).

Following what appears to have been the happy event of their marriage, another sad event took place at the end of the same year. On August 12, 1607 (*Comp Doc Life* 29), Shakespeare's youngest brother by sixteen years, Edmund, died at the age of twenty-seven, "shortly after the death of an illegitimate son, and the poet paid 20 shillings for his interment in the church of St. Savior's, Southwark" (Mutschmann and Wentersdorf 192). According to M. M. Reese, "his passing" was "marked by 'a forenoon knell of the great bell' " (249). The cost for this was 8s.

Six months later, in 1608, the year the King's Men players assumed the lease of the Blackfriars Theater, when Shakespeare was but forty-four, his first grandchild, Elizabeth Hall, was born and baptized on February 21. In April of that year, his brother-in-law was sworn in as church warden in the Stratford parish. On September 9 (one day after the seventh anniversary of her husband's death), his mother died: "Mary Shaxspere wydowe." And in the next month, October 16, 1608, Shakespeare participated in still another "family" role, standing as godfather at the baptism of William Walker, his name-child, son of Henry Walker, a Stratford alderman elected in 1606 (Gray 165).

Within the following two to three years he must still have taken an active part in Stratford since in 1608–9 his name was in the Stratford records as having sued a John Addenbrooke for debt. Yet in 1609 *Troilus and Cressida* was published (*Comp Doc Life* 267), indicating that he may have been in London as well.

However, by 1610 Shakespeare is generally thought to have been residing for the most part in Stratford. During the following two years, he lost his two remaining brothers, Gilbert ("who had taken legal delivery of his brother's purchase in Old Stratford" [Reese 249]), buried

February 3, 1612, and Richard, buried on February 4, 1613. Of the eight children born to John and Mary Shakespeare only William and his sister now survived, three of the girls having died in infancy. In 1612 he was in London as a witness in the Belott v. Mountjoy case: an action for the payment of dowry (*Doc Life* 211). In this court appearance he identified himself as being of Stratford-upon-Avon, indicating that he had retired to Stratford (Bentley 80). The following month, in March 1613, Shakespeare purchased the Blackfriars gatehouse, the last investment he made in London (*Comp Doc Life* 272). Only three months later, in June, the Globe burned to the ground (Gray 129).

In 1614, according to the Lord Chamberlain's accounts, "a preacher, one of the religious propagandists of the day, was entertained at New Place: Item, for on quart of sack, and on quart of clarrett winne, geven to a precher at the New Place, xx.d." Halliwell-Phillipps claims that he "was received at Stratford under the sanction of a Puritanical Corporation, and was entertained partly at their expense at Shakespeare's residence, a circumstance which shows at how early a period his family were turning their attention to serious subjects" (H-P, *Life* 225–26). The minds of most Stratfordians must have turned to serious thoughts that summer of 1614, for there was a calamitous fire on July 9. John Combe died the next day, leaving Shakespeare that £5 of which we have spoken before. By October Shakespeare became further involved in Stratford concerns when he entered into a dispute over enclosures that would further alter the face of the town.

The final recorded occasions of his presence in Stratford are the will itself, dated March 1616, and the entry in the church burial records of April 1616, following his death on April 23, probably his fifty-second birthday (he was born between April 20 and 26).

In reviewing these series of events in Shakespeare's final years, one must also keep in mind that they involved Anne as well. They were married to the end as the will confirms in the "infamous" interlineation "unto my wief. . . ." Anne's experience of family crises was not mitigated by distance as her husband's may often have been. As Schoenbaum has noted, "So far as is known, his wife never strayed from the town, but for her the record is a blank between the baptism of her children and the drawing up of the poet's will" (*Doc Life* 234). However, even in 1601, there is proof that there was no question in the minds of others in Stratford that she was Shakespeare's wife. Thomas Whittington, in his will of March 25, 1601, bequeathed to the poor of Stratford forty shillings "that is in the hand of Anne Shaxspere wyfe unto Mr. Wyllyam Shaxspere.'' A Thomas Whittington was described in the will of Richard Hathaway, Anne's father, as ''my sheepherd'' (Gray 160).

A great deal has been made of their having been married by the Bishop of Worcester, after only one asking of the banns, and of the added complication that the register lists an Ann Whateley of Temple Grafton as having been granted a license to marry W. Shakespeare, though there is no evidence that the dramatist was married there. Of Anne and William's daughter's having been born only six months later, it seems highly unlikely that there was any shame attached to these facts or to the early birth, since the girl was baptized at Holy Trinity church on the Sunday that was the feast day of the parish, May 26, 1583 (*Rec & Images* 75). The English customs of that time are noteworthy in this context. As Peter Alexander explains in *Shakespeare's Life and Art,*[4] marriage ''required neither church, nor priest, nor document of any kind, only the declaration of the contracting parties in the presence of witnesses. Such a marriage was recognized by Church and State, and reflected in no way on the respectability of the man and woman. It was customary, though not necessary, to follow the marriage proper at a convenient season by a ceremony in church.'' Certainly, as Martin Ingram brings out in his study *Church Courts, Sex and Marriage in England, 1570–1640,* based on many of the court records of the period, ''Attitudes to antenuptial fornication are best summed up as ambivalent but, especially before the end of Elizabeth's reign, tending toward tolerance,'' although ''little shame or disgrace seems to have been attached to bridal pregnancy'' (230).

Swinburne here again proves to be a major source. In *The Treatise* he makes direct reference to the unquestionable legality of the solemnity of marriage even without bans. In fact, he draws from it an analogy to explain his contention regarding the remaining force of the Solemn Testament even though the Unsolemn was the more generally recognized by that time. This passage is of special interest for the light it sheds on Shakespeare's own marriage and the legality of Anne's dower rights:

> For as an unsolemne marriage is not therefore no marriage because it is unsolemne, (the banes perhapes not being published, or the marriage not being celebrated in the face of the Church, but privately in a Chamber, or some other rite or ceremonie thereof being omitted) [as was the case for Shakespeare and his bride] but is neverthelesse reputed for a true marriage: (So that the same were solemnized by a Minister in the presence of a sufficient number of persons therunto required, by whose tes-

> timony the same might be proved; in which case the said marriage may be said to be celebrated in the face of the Church, though neither in Church nor Chappell, but in a chamber, none being seriously or purposely excluded.) Both in the Ecclesiasticall Courts, in respect of the knot or essence of matrimonies & in temporall Courts, in respect of the wives dower, and other Legall effects: At least if the parties married be licensed or dispensed with by the Ordinary in that behalfe: . . . So that there be no other lawful impediment . . . but the defect of solemnity onely. (1611, 21-23 / E4-E6; 1590, 18^{v}–20^{v} / no signature until 21 = E)

Assuming that her pregnancy lasted nine months, Anne became pregnant in the month following the probation of her father's will. Anne's father died the year she and William married; his will was probated on July 9, 1582. His daughter, Agnes, or Anne, was to get £6 13 *s.* 4 *d.* "to be paide unto her at the daie of her marriage" (which she was duly given). Thomas, his second son, had two children named in this will, the first one named Agnes (perhaps for her aunt), each of whom got a sheep (Gray 221–23). According to *Tithes & Oblations,* the bequest of lambs by fathers to daughters is not counted as part of his tithe; they belong to her, i.e., "is their owne" (27).

Before Anne Shakespeare died, seven years after her husband, on August 6, 1623, at the age of sixty-seven, she expressed a desire to be buried in the same grave as her husband, but out of respect for the plea of the epitaph she declined to open it and rests instead to the left of him, *between* [my italics] him and the northern wall (Mutschmann and Wentersdorf, 201). John Dowdall, on visiting Shakespeare's tomb in 1693, wrote: " 'Not one for feare of the Curse aboves^{d} Dare Touch his Grave Stone tho his wife and Daughters Did earnestly Desire to be Layd in the same Grave wth him' " (Gray 75).

Anne's epitaph, attributed to their first-born child, Susanna, certainly inclines one away from the view of either unsound mind or unpleasantness of character:

> Ubera tu mater, tu lac, vitamque dedisti,
> Vae mihi pro tanto munere saxa dabo,
> Quam mallem amoveat lapidem bonus Angelus ore,
> Exeat ut Christi corpus imago tua;
> Sed nil vota valent, venias cito Christe, resurget,
> Clausa licet tumulo mater et astra petet.[5]

> [Thou my mother gavest me life, thy breast and milk; alas, for such great bounty to me I shall give thee a stone; how much rather I would entreat

> the good angel to move the stone, so that thy figure might come forth, as did the Body of Christ. But my prayers avail nothing. Come quickly, O Christ. My mother lies closed in the tomb; she will rise again and seek the stars.][6]

At any rate Anne raised the three children largely as a single parent (Shakespeare having left Stratford in anywhere from 1582 to as late as 1592),[7] until 1608, when her husband appears to have resettled in permanent residence (though still traveling to London on certain occasions).

Scholars have created a story of estrangement, but Gray for one has noted that "some weightier motive than content with the fortune he had accumulated or the mere desire for a peaceful life at Stratford" must account for Shakespeare's decision "to abandon in his prime the occupations and pleasures which for more than twenty-five years had filled his life" (132). The will stands as an incontestably family-centered document, not only in the poet's own family but, as I have shown, related to the Combe and Walker families as well. Even for the year 1614, when, as we have seen, it is recorded that he was in Stratford entering disputes over enclosures, it is also recorded he was in London. But note that, for the family side of the record, he was travelling with his son-in-law John Hall (Eccles 140).

Of course he apparently returned often enough, for John Aubrey tells us, "He was wont to goe to his native countrey once a yeare" (225–27; Gray 72). And certainly frequent travel to London was not out of the question. As his contemporary Richard Quiney informs us of the journey between Stratford and London, it took only six days "going thither and coming homewards," riding up "by way of Oxford, High Wycombe, and Uxbridge, and home through Aylesbury and Banbury" (Eccles 97).

To judge from the recorded evidence and the crucial events previously recounted, Shakespeare would have to have been indefatigable during the final period of his life, traveling often between Stratford and London. There is no record of his having held town office as he would almost certainly have done had he been residing most of the time in Stratford. Besides, no fewer than twenty-four plays have been assigned dates of composition during these years, the last eight of which, significantly, deal with variations on a theme of family reunion.[8]

The preoccupation with family is a distinguishing mark of the last plays. As Margaret Loftus Ranald has brought out, "Marriage is the one human relationship portrayed in almost every play and almost every poem.'' Yet as Professor Ranald further observes, ''By the last plays Shakespeare lessens his emphasis on matrimonial law, developing his treatment of marriage far beyond the use of legalism as a major plot device or as realistic detail. He now celebrates love, the kind of virtuous love that ends in marriage, the fertile relationship that purifies and ennobles humankind'' (81).

Shakespeare's life is always being ''read'' into the plays. Readers, ever avid in pursuit of the artist elusively barricaded within the aesthetic walls of his art, have drawn all sorts of parallels between Shakespeare's life and the plays, even interpreting them on the basis of biography, factual or otherwise. The marriage of Susanna has been seen in *King Lear;* thc birth of his granddaughter, Elizabeth Hall, in the passage on the birth of Queen Elizabeth in *Henry VIII* (Knight 249–51); Hamnet's age in that of Prince Mamillius of *The Winter's Tale,* just a little more than eleven years at the time of his death (French 379). The span of sixteen years between Hermione's ''death'' and final reconciliation with her husband may be compared to the interim between Shakespeare's departure from Stratford (if it was anywhere between c.1591–92) and return in 1608; and perhaps something of his wife Anne's suffering over the loss of their son may be echoed in the inconsolable sorrow expressed by both Hermione in *The Winter's Tale* (''That honorable grief lodg'd here which burns / Worse than tears drown,'' II.i.108), and in *King John* (''Grief fills the room up of my absent child,'' III.iv.93), an interpretation to which we may be inclined to give more credence because it is an early play.

Yet this line of thinking, while intriguing, in the end is lacking in conclusive proof and has led to some often unbridled speculation bordering on idolization. This approach to Shakespearean study has been indicted by G. K. Chesterton as ''the messiahship of Shakespeare.'' It seems bent upon ''turning good poetry into bad metaphysics,'' according to Chesterton: ''Shakespeare was in one sense a thorough mystic; he saw in every stone in the street things which cannot be uttered till the end of the world. His Perdita is not 'a type of the Reformation' but simply a girl in love; the Reformation is, in comparison, a trivial thing.''[9]

Shakespeare's realistic outlook is evident even in the will, where each bequest seems to have been made in an extraordinarily focused consideration of the particular person's life situation. The recipients are emphasized over the bequests. Moreover, the airtight legalities of the will further demonstrate an astute, pragmatic perception, one which we have every reason to assume was Shakespeare's as the devisement obviously reflects his dispositions of property and goods. His approach in the will, whether in regard to family, friends, property, or law, was both realistic and practical.

My purpose here is to show that the one connection which can be irrefutably made between the poet's will and his last plays is an almost total (might one suggest converging?) emphasis on family. As Peter Alexander observes in *Shakespeare's Life and Art,* "The will shows the understanding and harmony that must have prevailed in the home" (224). In Shakespeare's later years, family concerns were at the forefront in the two major areas of his experience, both in his personal life at Stratford and in his playwriting for the London stage. In this context one gains a culminating view of Shakespeare's will as a family document.

Civil law confirms the will as a protective gesture on the dramatist's part, as an unequivocal declaration of privacy. The religious character of the will, while not prejudicial for or against any denominational persuasion, does nevertheless avow Christianity as does Shakespeare's careful preparation for perpetual entombment at the foot of the altar of Holy Trinity Church, where on the twenty-fifth, two days after his death, as was the custom, he was buried near the northern wall of the church in a grave inside the chancel—significantly, the customary burial place of the owners of the tithes.

Over the centuries, laws and customs pass into disuse and are forgotten. Brought to light again, they recreate the context of their time. They extend our understanding beyond limits imposed by our own narrow historical perspective. Recovering the intent of the law and custom operative in Shakespeare's will brings us to a greater appreciation of the man's deliberation in ordering his life and honoring his life ties in a final act of provision and farewell.

Notes

PREFACE

1. Readers interested in the subject are referred to Phillips' ample bibliography in *Shakespeare and the Lawyers* (London: Methuen, 1972) 193–210.

2. E. D. Hirsch, Jr., *Validity in Interpretation* (New Haven & London: Yale University Press, 1967) vii.

CHAPTER ONE

1. Vertue, British Library, MS. Portland Loan 29/246, p. 19, quoted in S. Schoenbaum, *William Shakespeare: A Documentary Life* [hereafter abbreviated *Doc Life*] (Oxford: Clarendon Press in association with the Scolar Press, 1975) 242.

2. "Doctors' Commons," *Encyclopedia Britannica,* 1988 ed.

3. Facsimiles are available in most of the comprehensive studies, e.g., E. K. Chambers, *William Shakespeare: A Study of Facts and Problems* [hereafter abbreviated EKC] (Oxford: Clarendon Press, 1930) vol. 2; B. Roland Lewis, *The Shakespeare Documents* [hereafter abbreviated BRL] (Stanford: Stanford University Press, and London: Oxford University Press, 1941) vol. 2; *Doc Life* 243–45; and most recently, *Shakespeare in the Public Records* [hereafter abbreviated *Sh/Pub Rec*], eds. David Thomas and Jane Cox (London: Her Majesty's Stationery Office, 1985). I have also found very useful for its demarcation of individual sheets and the *position* of Shakespeare's signature on each sheet the version transcribed into modern spelling by H. Mutschmann and K. Wentersdorf in *Shakespeare and Catholicism* (New York: Sheed and Ward, 1952) 404–9. I would also like to commend the prodigious efforts in transcribing the will by hand in the Pre-Fax days of the 1850s of the late T. Rodd and

the late J. O. Halliwell for presenting the work in the first transcription of the will "preserving the interlineations," in *Shakespeare's Will* (London: John Russell Smith, 1851).

4. Charles Hamilton gives the precise measurements as 12⅛″ × 15⅝″; 12½″ × 15¾″, and 12¼″ × 15⅜″, respectively (*In Search of Shakespeare: A Reconnaissance into the Poet's Life and Handwriting* [San Diego, New York, London: Harcourt Brace Jovanovich, 1985], 63).

5. M. M. Reese, *Shakespeare, His World and His Work* (London: Edward Arnold Publishers Ltd., 1953; rev. ed 1980) 253.

6. James O. Halliwell-Phillipps says that she was nine, in *The Life of Shakespere,* vol. 2 of *The Works of William Shakespere* [hereafter abbreviated *Life*] (London: C. and J. Adlard, 1853) 382.

7. Joan Hart outlived her brother by thirty years, dying on November 4, 1646 (*Doc Life* 273).

8. The insertion of the boy's name, *Thomas,* in the transcript copy of the original now called the "Birthplace Copy," has led to conjecture that it was likely to have been supplied by a family member, Shakespeare Hart, who, according to George Vertue, "had a copy of the will in his possession." See Frank Simpson, "New Place: The Only Representation of Shakespeare's House, from an Unpublished MS," *Shakespeare Survey* 5 (1952):57.

9. Mark Eccles, *Shakespeare in Warwickshire* (Madison: University of Wisconsin Press, 1961) 121. As Eccles points out, William Combe, John Combe's brother, was a lawyer admitted in 1571 to the Middle Temple, one of the Inns of Court in London where several of Shakespeare's plays were in fact produced. Combe was a reader there in 1595, although by 1597 he had become counsel for Stratford (102 f.).

10. *Shakespere: The Man and His Achievement* (London: J. M. Dent and Sons, 1977) 206.

11. Peter Levi, *The Life and Times of William Shakespeare* (London: Macmillan, 1988) 342.

12. Cf. Eccles 142, and S. Schoenbaum, *William Shakespeare: Records and Images* [hereafter abbreviated *Rec & Images*] (New York: Oxford University Press, 1981) 47.

13. Frank Marcham, *William Shakespeare and His Daughter Susannah* (London: Grafton & Co., 1931) 59.

14. George Russell French, *Shakespeareana Genealogica* (London and Cambridge: Macmillan, 1869) 281.

15. *Aubrey's Brief Lives,* ed. Oliver Lawson Dick (London: Secker and Warburg, 1949; rpt. Middlesex, England: Penguin Books, 1982) 334.

16. A. L. Rowse, *William Shakespeare: A Biography* (New York and Evanston: Harper and Row, 1963) 128–29.

17. William Dean Howells, *The Seen and Unseen at Stratford-on-Avon: A Fantasy* (New York: Harper & Bros., MCMXIV) 16.

18. Edward Wagenknecht, *The Personality of Shakespeare* (Norman: University of Oklahoma Press, 1972) 92.

19. Nicholas Rowe, quoted in BRL 2:271.

20. *Correspondence of the Reverend Joseph Greene: Parson, Schoolmaster, and Antiquary, 1712–1790,* ed. Levi Fox (London: Stationery Office, 1965) 59.

21. G. E. Bentley, *Shakespeare: A Biographical Handbook* (New Haven: 1961) 61, quoted in *Doc Life,* 246.

22. See E. B. Everitt, *The Young Shakespeare: Studies in Documentary Evidence* (Copenhagen: Rosenkilde and Bagger, 1954) 184–187, and Hamilton, 6.

23. Hugh A. Hanley, ''Shakespeare's Family in Stratford Records,'' *The Times Literary Supplement* (21 May, 1964):441.

24. John Rudstone, *An Almanacke and Prognostication for the yeere of our Lord God 1616* (London: Stationer's Co., 1616) n.p. [Bodleian Ash. 65]. The year 1616 was regarded as an auspicious one for being a leap year, ''the Bissextile or leape yeare,'' according to Augustine Upcote, ''gentleman, student of physicke and mathematickes,'' *An Almanacke and Prognostication for this yeare of our Lord God 1616. Being the Bissextile or leape yeare* (London: Stationer's Co., 1616) n.p. [Bodleian Ash. 65]. Easter that year was on March 31, by the ''old account'' (on April 3 by the ''new reformed account used beyond the seas by ship's navigators [Rudstone, n.p.]). See also William Dade, Gentleman practitioner in Phisick, *A New Almanacke and Prognostication, with the FOIRAINE Computation, in which you may behold the state of this yeare of our Lord God 1616. Being Leape yeare* (London: Stationer's Co., 1616) n.p. So it was on the Monday of Holy Week that the will was altered, Thomas Bretnor, [''Professour of the Mathematicks & Student in Physicke''], *A Newe Almanacke and Prognostication for the yeare of our Lord God, 1616* (London: Stationer's Co., 1616) C-4. At that time, according to Schoenbaum, the year in England then ''began officially on'' March 25, also known as ''Lady Day,'' after the feast of the Annunciation of Mary celebrated on that day (*Comp Doc Life* xiii). Feasts celebrated on the three days central to the will and Shakespeare's death, as designated by Rudstone, were: January 25, the Conversion of Paul; March 25, the Annunciation of Mary; and April 23, the day Shakespeare died, the feast of St. George, patron of England.

Shakespeare's grave lies at the foot of the high altar in Stratford's Church of the Holy Trinity, on the left side, directly in line with the figure that depicts St. George in the stained glass windows behind and just above the altar.

25. Charles Elton, K. C., *William Shakespeare: His Family and Friends,* 227–30, quoted in Green, 11.

26. Hamilton points out that Chambers noticed that the ink of the interlinear insertions was different from that used in writing the body of the will, and that

Tannenbaum noted that the ink of the interlinear corrections was the same as the ink used by the witnesses (76).

27. (London: John Windet, 1568 [4° R of Th. Douce SS111, Bodleian Library Catalogue]; 2nd ed. 1590 [4° A. 30 Jur. Bodleian Library Catalogue] London: Stationers' 1611, 1635.)

28. *Sh/Pub Rec* 24. The name is spelled "Swinburne" at the end of the prefatory letter of the 1611 edition even though it is "Swinburn" on the title page, reflecting the inconsistency in Elizabethan spelling practices. Folios 8–9, 188, and 215–17 are misnumbered; 10, 108, and 218–23 are missing in number only. In the 1611 edition the Written Testament is in the fourth part, sec. 25. B. Roland Lewis, too, cites Swinburne's 1611 edition as "the reliable, critical treatise on Elizabethan wills" (2:492, n. 26).

CHAPTER TWO

1. James O. Halliwell-Phillips, *The Life of William Shakespeare: Abbreviated* [hereafter abbreviated *Life Abb*] (New York: Bigelow Smith, 1909) 174.

2. "The decline of ecclesiastical jurisdiction under the Tudors," in *Continuity and Change: Personnel and Administration of the Church in England 1500–1642,* eds. Felicity Heal and Rosemary O'Day (London: Leicester University Press, 1976) 246.

3. *Outlines of the Life of Shakespeare* [hereafter abbreviated *Outlines*] vol. I, 10th ed. (London, New York, Bombay: Longmans, Green, 1898) 252.

4. *Corpus Juris Civilis* ("De Testamentis Ordinandis," *Institutiones* X, 17).

5. In sharp contrast to its predecessor, the *Leges Henrici,* this was the "the first of the legal classics" of England and, according to Heinrich Brunner, "The Sources of English Law," in *Select Essays in Anglo-American Legal History* [hereafter abbreviated *SEAALH*], vol. 2 (Boston: Little, Brown, 1909) 34, "The first attempt at a scientific exposition of native law in modern Europe." So singular is it that it is always referred to as "Glanvill." Glanvill died a Crusader at the siege of Acre in 1190.

6. F. G. Emmison, *Elizabethan Life: Home, Work, and Land* (Chelmsford: Essex County Council, and Plymouth, Mass.: Pilgrim Society and Plimoth Plantation, 1976) 107.

7. John Rastell, *An Exposition of Certaine Difficult and Obscure Words, and Termes of the Lawes of This Realme . . . unto are also added the Old Tenures* (London: Richard Tottell, 1572; 1579; 1592; 1598; 1609) fols. 40; 201–2; 72a; and 172, respectively.

8. Sidney Lee, *A Life of William Shakespeare,* 4th ed. (revised version, 1925) 488–89.

9. Dorothy Whitelock, ed. *Anglo-Saxon Wills* (Cambridge: Cambridge University Press, 1930) 82; see also "Changing Currents in Anglo-Saxon Studies," in *History, Law and Literature in 10th–11th Century England* [hereafter abbreviated *HLL*] (London: Variorum Reprints, 1981) 82 (line 6).

10. Henry Bracton, *De Legibus et Consuetudinibus Angliae (1640): Bracton on the Laws and Customs of England,* trans. and rev. Samuel E. Thorne, 2 vols., Vol. 2 (Cambridge, MA.: Belknap Press of Harvard University Press, published in Association with the Selden Society, 1968) 265. See also Sir Frederick Pollock and Frederic William Maitland, *The History of English Law Before the Time of Edward I* [hereafter abbreviated Pol & Mait], 2nd ed. (Cambridge: Univ. Press, 1968) 425, n. 4. Born Henry de Bratton, he was a clergyman and royal judge under Henry III (1216–72). According to W. R. Jones in "The Two Laws in England: The Later Middle Ages," *Traditio* XI (1969):111–31, Bracton "was once archdeacon of Barn staple and trained in the canons" (121). He cites the incorrect spelling of his name by which he has come down to posterity as "an illustration of the invalidity of a writ" for it was "frequently misspelled by copyists" (see Brunner, "The Sources of English Law," *SEAALH,* 2:35). Maitland regarded Bracton's work as "the crown and flower of English mediaeval jurisprudence," quoted in Brunner, 35.

11. *Commentaries* 2:iii and v. I used the London 1800 ed. as well.

12. *The Calendar of Wills* A.D. *1258*–A.D. *1688, Part II:* A.D. *1358*–A.D. *1688,* ed. Reginald R. Sharpe (London: John C. Francis, 1890) 682.

13. *Test Papers* 6. That Shakespeare appears to have been fascinated with legal quibbles and complications linked to English matrimonial law in *All's Well That Ends Well* and *Measure for Measure,* has been shown by Margaret Loftus Ranald in " 'As Marriage Binds, and Blood Breaks': English Marriage and Shakespeare," *Shakespeare Quarterly* 30 (Winter 1979):69–70, n.4: "As a result of the institution of the jointure, wives did not have to be mentioned in the wills of their husbands, unless some unusual bequest was made. Such may have been the case of Shakespeare's 'second-best bed.' The Church also used the wife's right to dower as a means of preventing clandestine marriages, because such financial arrangements were officially made 'atte churche dore' before the ceremony 'in facie ecclesiae.' "

CHAPTER THREE

1. W. H. Elton, "Shakespeare and the thought of his age," in *The Cambridge Companion to Shakespeare Studies,* ed. Stanley Wells (Cambridge: Cambridge University Press, 1986) 17.

2. (Cambridge: Cambridge University Press, 1987; repr. 1988) 42.

3. William Harrison, quoted in Bertil Johansson, *Law and Lawyers in Elizabethan England* (Stockholm: Almquist & Wiksell, 1967) n. 11, 8.

4. William K. Boyd, "The Ecclesiastical Edicts of the Theodosian Code," *Studies in History, Economics, and Public Law,* Vol. 24, no. 63 (New York: Columbia University Press, 1905) 91.

5. George Keeton, *English Law: The Judicial Contribution* (New Abbot & Devon: David & Charles, 1974) 58.

6. J. A. Clarence Smith, *Medieval Law Teachers and Writers, Civilian and*

Canonist (Ottawa, Canada: University of Ottawa Press, 1975) 118. In his recent study, *Roman Canon Law in the Reformation* (Cambridge: Cambridge University Press, 1990), R. H. Helmholz makes the point that ''the closure of the canon law faculties at Oxford and Cambridge'' may not have ''ended all study of canon law there'' (152).

7. Richard M. Wunderli, *London Church Courts and Society on the Eve of the Reformation* (Cambridge, Mass.: Medieval Academy of America, 1981) 137.

8. Plucknett, ''Consuetudines Diversarum Curiarum,'' in *Select Proceedings without Writ,* Vol. 60 (Selden Society, n.d.) cxcv–cciii.

9. Richard Cosin, *Apologie of and for Sundrie Proceedings by Jurisdiction Ecclesiasticall, of late times by some challenged, and also diversly by them impugned* (London, 1591).

10. Sir William Dugdale, *Monasticon Anglicanum: A History of the Abbies and Other Monasteries, Hospitals, Frieries, and Cathedral and 38 Collegiate Churches with their Dependencies in England and Wales.* trans. and ed. John Caley et al. (London: Longman, 1817–19), 1:567. Of interest with regard to the historically strong Catholic character of the Stratford ecclesiastical jurisdiction is Dugdale's notation about the prioress of a Benedictine nunnery at Wroxhall, also spelled Wrocheshale, in Warwickshire, near Killecote (or Kaldecote), who might possibly have been a distant relative of Shakespeare's: ''Licentia concessa fuit Johannae Shakespere sub priorissae ad eligend. 5 Sept. 1525. et 20 Nov. 1525 Agnes Litle confirmata fuit priorissa [*sic*] de Wroxhall, vac. per resign. Joc Brome'' (4:88–89). This estate was ultimately purchased in 1713 by Sir Christopher Wren; it had been founded by Hugh, the son of Richard, lord of Hatton, in the reign of Edward III, as a fulfillment of a visitation from St. Leonard, the patron of the church in their parish church (4:90).

11. Geoffrey Rudolph Elton, *England, 1200–1640: The Sources of History* (Ithaca: Cornell University Press, 1969) 105–6.

12. See Felicity Heal and Rosemary O'Day, ''Clerical Tax Collection under the Tudors: The Influence of the Reformation,'' in Heal and O'Day, eds., *Continuity and Change: Personnel and Administration of the Church in England 1500–1642* (London: Leicester University Press, 1976) 97–125.

13. C. W. Brooks, *Pettyfoggers and Vipers of the Commonwealth: The 'Lower Branch' of the Legal Profession in Early Modern England* (Cambridge: Cambridge University Press, 1986) 75.

14. A. C. Southern, *Elizabethan Recusant Prose, 1559–1582* (London: Sands, 1950) 21.

15. For a detailed report on the development of the society, see Joseph M. Levine, ''Tudor Antiquaries,'' *History Today* 20 (1970):278–85.

16. William Lambarde, *APXAIONOMIA, sive De Priscis Anglorum legibus,* Saxon. et Lat. (London: John Davis, 1568); Folger Shakespeare Library, 1568, microfilm of Shakespeare signature copy. Hamilton disputes the authenticity of

the signature even though, as he points out, "the script was tested at the National Archives and results conclusively established that the ink was of the Elizabethan era" (240).

17. "Early Anglo-Saxon Studies and Legal Scholarship in the Renaissance," *Studies in the Renaissance* 5(1958):104.

18. Laurence Nowell, *Vocabularium Saxonicum,* ed. Albert H. Marckwardt (Ann Arbor: University of Michigan Press, 1952) 17. See also J. Q. Adams, "A New Signature of Shakespeare?" *Bulletin of the John Rylands Library, Manchester* 27 (1943):256–59.

19. Giles E. Dawson, "Authenticity and Attribution of Written Matter," *English Institute Annual* (1942) (New York: Columbia University Press, 1943) 100. For a detailed account of the analysis and claims for and against the authenticity of this signature, see *Rec & Images,* 104–9. Professor Schoenbaum supports the conclusion of Giles E. Dawson that "there is a better chance that the signature is genuine than that it is not," but adds, "The Lambarde signature makes a better claim to authenticity than any other pretended Shakespeare autograph but it is premature, to say the least, to classify it as the poet's seventh signature" (109). I should like to make clear that while I am aware of W. Nicholas Knight's book, *Shakespeare's Hidden Life: Shakespeare at the Law 1585–1595* (New York: Mason and Lipscomb, 1973), and even refer to it where it has seemed appropriate to do so, neither my interest in the *Archaionomia* nor any part of my study is in any way related to or dependent upon his conjectures.

20. Wilbur Dunkel, *William Lambarde, Elizabethan Jurist, 1536–1601* (New Brunswick: Rutgers University Press, 1965) 35. Scholarship of our day, however, has uncovered many errors in the Anglo-Saxon transcription (see Kenneth Sisam on the specific errors and Elizabethan renderings of the Old English supplied by Nowell and/or Lambarde, "not with intention to deceive," in *Studies in the History of Old English Literature* [Oxford: Clarendon Press, 1953] 232–58).

21. In the *Vocabularium Saxonicum* Nowell defined *cyricsceat* as "Certayne money due to the curche" (53); *sawul* as "A soule" (143); and *sceat* as "money, treasure, rent. *Cyricsceat.* Money due to the churche. Medsceatas. Bribes, rewardes. Deorwyr sceattas" (144), to which Lambarde added "Sceatta. A pece of money whereof 30 made 120 poundes, after some. . . . Other places seeme to make it small money" (144).

> Et quod non dimittitur peccatum nisi restituatur ablatum, prudenter attendens: salubriter statuit, quod prorecompensatione decimarum taliter subtractarum, licet suo statuto cansam non infeeruit, secundum melius animal defuncti Ecclesiae damnum passae debuit applicari. Quia vero hujusmodi occasione statuti inter rectores / celesiarum & parochianos suos lites, quas extingui cupimus, frequentius oriuntur: illud duximus synodali interpretatione declarandum, quod si decedens tria tantummodo vel plura cujuscunque generis in bonis suis habuerit animalia,

(optimo domino cui de jure sue it debitum reservato) Ecclesiae suae, a qua Sacramenta recepit, dum vivetet, sine dolo, fraude, & contradictione qualibet pro recompensatione subtractionis decimarum tam personalium quam praedialium, necnon oblationum, ad liberationem animae suae, melius animal post optimum reservertur.

[Regarding the statement that the sin is not forgiven without restitution of the stolen object [take] the following in close consideration. He justly decided that for the repaying of the tithes so removed even if he did not allege any excuse, accordingly the best animal must be given to the defrauded church of the defunct person. This decree is a frequent cause of various disagreements, to which we would like to put a stop, between pastors and parishioners. Backed by the consensus of the synod we brought up that famous principle that if the deceased had among his possessions only three or several animals of different species (which *de jure* belong to the good lord) he must set aside the best animal for the Church from which he receives the Sacraments; he must do it while alive without cunning or fraud or other reservations in order to compensate for what he stole of the tithings either in personal or real property. He must also make offerings; all this in order to save his soul].

The reader should know about two unprinted manuscripts cited in Helmholz (134, fns. 44 & 45), which was published just as my study was in the final stages of completion. I could not consult these manuscripts as they are in the British Library, one pertaining to the law of tithes (fn.44: BL Lansd. MS. 132, fols. 164–90v) and the other on testamentary law (Cotton MS. Cleo F.I, fols. 338–434, p. 134).

22. Peter Milward, *Shakespeare's Religious Background* (London: Sidgwick and Jackson, 1973) 20–22. (A reprint of the 1638 English text is included in James G. McManaway, "John Shakespeare's 'Spiritual Testament,' *Shakespeare Quarterly* 18 [1967]:197–205.) J. Tom Burgess (*Historic Warwickshire,* ed. Joseph Hill, 2d ed. [Birmingham: 1893]), believed the character of Isabella to be "an embodiment of his reverence for the memory of Isabella Shakespeare 'quondam prioressa' of the neighboring nunnery" (295). George Russell French found that a Richard Shakespeare was a tenant of the monastery, holding a cottage with its appurtenances in the lordship of Wroxhall in 1536. Three other Shakespeares "are assessed in the small sums at Wroxhall, all of whom were named William" (354–55); and a Roger Shakspere was a monk at Bordesley Monastery "to whom at its dissolution was granted an annuity of one hundred shillings" (357). (We have already noted Dugdale's reference to the nun Johannae Shakespere of Wroxhall.) Burgess gives the entire account of the legend of the miraculous deliverance of Hugh from captivity in the Holy Land to his own Wroxhall woods and his vow to found there a house of nuns of St. Benet's order. On the preponderance of Catholics or Catholic sympathizers represented in the will, and John Robinson, tenant of Shakespeare's Gatehouse at Blackfriars, see Mutschmann and Wentersdorf, 191–93. See also Williams and Chambers, *A Short Life of William Shakespeare* 14 ff.

23. (Manchester, U.K., and Dover, New Hampshire: Manchester University Press, 1985) 116.

24. *EKC,* 11.

25. French, "Notes on the Shakespeare & Arden Families," *Shakespeareana Genealogica,* Table II, The Poet's Family, 383. Chambers also presents a detailed tracing of family history, 2:48 ff.

26. E. R. C. Brinkworth, *Shakespeare and the Bawdy Court of Stratford* (London and Chichester: Phillimore, 1972) 5. R. J. Schoeck, who has contributed enormously to laying the bibliographical foundations in this field, maintains that "any attempt to understand early Tudor history or political thought without considering the theories and discussions of the canonists is incomplete, if not fruitless; for the influence of the canon law in pre-Reformation England was immensely far-reaching and immensely significant" ("Canon Law in England on the Eve of the Reformation," *Mediaeval Studies,* 25 [1963]:147).

27. Henry Swinburne, *A Treatise of Spousals, or Matrimonial Contracts; Wherein All the Questions relating to that Subject are ingeniously Debated and Resolved.* (London: S. Roycroft for Robert Clavell, 1606, 1686) 5–8, 45, 47.

28. No less rich a source are the cases, or "stories," cited in books on the laws. The clusters of details here that find their parallels in Shakespeare's plays are just too remarkable to be ignored. For example, in Swinburne's *The fourth part of the formes of testamentes,* reference is made to the law of legitimacy which declared that even if "the childe bee verie like the adulterer, yet shall the husbande bee deemed the father. Wherein diverse (I confesse) of no small aucthoritie have contended mightilie, that this childe is to bee adiuged the adulterers, fortifying their assertion with this reason especially, because in other creatures nature hath so provided, that each thing dooth beget that which is like unto it self." Swinburne gives as precedent to this position "a well-known story." One thinks of *Othello* in reading the story:

> Famous also is that accident (registered in the bookes of sundrie writers) of a beautifull ladie, who having a husband of a faire and white complexion, was delivered of a childe as blacke as pitch, like unto a Moore or Ethiopian: and hereupon being accused of adulterie, shee was acquited and absolved, for that by the opinion of the best learned in phisicke and philosophie, the same did so come to passe by reason of the picture of a black boie, or like Nigro, which did hang in the bedchamber at the time of the conception. (1590, 152–64/Y6–Y7; 1611, 172/Bb4 ff.)

Another case to which Swinburne alludes, in connection with the power of the woman's imagination in "the act of generation," contains a juxtaposition of elements common to *The Winter's Tale.*

> Like unto this is that credible historie of another woman in the time of Charles the fourth, Emperour and king of Boemia, who because she had too much regard to the picture of Saint John clothed in a Camels skinne, which did hang at the

> beds feete during the conception, shee brought foorth a childe all rough, covered with haire like unto a Beare. The histories are full of these kinde of accidents, I shall content myself with one more, which did befall in the time of the Emperour Maximilian, in a towne in Brabant: There in a publike plaie or spectacle, a certaine man whose part was to plaie a dauncing devill, assoone as the plaie was ended, ranne home to his wife in his devils attire: and being moved in spirit, catched his wife hastilie in his armes, and muste needes &c. in that habite, saying he would beget a devill; and so it came to passe, that at her childes birth shee was delivered of a devilish monster, which as soone as it was borne, began to leape and daunce like to the father. (1590, Y7^{v}; 1611, Bb4 ff.)

The study of laws and acts of the courts will prove to be not only fruitful but indispensable to scholarship.

29. Darryl Gless, *"Measure for Measure," the Law, and the Convent* (Princeton, N.J.: Princeton University Press, 1979).

30. For a full-length study of Thomas Russell and his relationship with Shakespeare, see Leslie Hotson, *I, William Shakespere* (London: Jonathan Cape, 1937).

CHAPTER FOUR

1. See Leslie Steevens in S. Schoenbaum, *Shakespeare's Lives* [hereafter abbreviated *Sh's Lives*] (Oxford: Clarendon Press, and New York: Oxford University Press, 1970) 174. In 1811 Nathan Drake also proffered the opinion "that nothing harsh or unjust had been committed by him on this occasion" (272). An anonymous critic of this period conjectured that "the second-best bed probably had more affectionate associations than the first and may have served on the wedding night" (311).

2. Quoted in *Doc Life* 247–48. Malone held that Shakespeare deliberately omitted her name from the will, pointing out that "the bitter sarcasm of the bequest by which he remembers afterward" demonstrates his "unfriendly feelings toward her," quoted in *Sh's Lives* 307.

3. *The Pictorial Edition of the Works of Shakspere,* vol. 2, 192, quoted in Phillips, 16–7.

4. The *depositio* was the section of provisions of bequest; the *sanctio* was the witnessing. Although Lewis offers a sound analysis of the form of the will, his observations that a bequest was "seldom . . . made via a wife" but rather "through a son (oldest son) or else through a male kinsman," and that "Dower, in the modern conventional idea of one-third to the wife, was virtually unknown" (475), simply are not borne out by the majority of wills of the time.

5. In its continuation of marked features such as this in the notification and its "links to the Adieu form," Eber Carle Perrow claimed the testament became "a favorite form of literature" during the later Middle Ages in Western Europe and especially in France and England, a "vogue that began in the fourteenth and fifteenth centuries and continued until as late as the eighteenth cen-

tury'' (705), in ''The Last Will and Testament as a Form of Literature,'' *Transactions of the Wisconsin Academy of Sciences, Arts and Letters* 17, 1 (1914) 705 ff. Perrow cites eight instances of allusion to the testament as a literary form in Shakespeare: RLuc 11. 1181–1211; RichII III,ii,148; MW V,v 27; ASLI II,i,47; IV,iv,192; TC V,x,51; Per I,i,47; AC V,ii,292; and WT V,iii,102.

6. *OED*

7. Frederick J. Furnivall, ed. *Earliest English Wills* in the Court of Probate, London: A.D. 1387–1439; with a priest's of 1454, No. 78, Early English Text Society [EETS] (London: Trubner, 1882) 114.

8. Charles Williams, *A Short Life of Shakespeare,* an abridgement of E. K. Chambers, *William Shakespeare: A Study of Facts and Problems* (Oxford: Oxford University Press, n.d.) 166.

9. Sir Edward Coke, *Commentarie upon Littleton* (1629), quoted in H-P, *Outlines* 392. Chief Justice Coke's great contribution to English legal history was the *Institutes of the Laws of England,* which he brought out in 1628. Until he lost the king's favor in 1616 partly as a consequence of the antagonism of his opponent, Francis Bacon, he served as attorney general (1594) and chief justice first of the Common Pleas (1606) and then of the King's Bench (1613) (Brunner, *SEAALH* 2:48).

10. Doris M. Stenton, *The English Woman in History* (London: Allen and Unwin; New York: Macmillan, 1957) 21.

11. Benjamin Thorpe, *The Ancient Laws and Institutes of England,* Vol. 2 (London: Records Commission, 1840), p. 317 by Dr. Bosworth's numbering in his personal copy now held by the Oxford University Law Library. See also *Hist Eng Law* 2:90, 92–93.

12. (London: Richard Tottell, 1572; 1579; 1592; 1598; 1609) Fol. 136.

13. *Commentaries* 2:425, and William Lyndwood, *Provinciale (Constitutions of Lambeth)* (Oxford: Hall and Davis, 1679) fol. T.C.I, 345.

14. *Middle English Dictionary,* ed. Sherman Kuhn, Vol. 7 (Ann Arbor: University of Michigan Press, 1975) 708. *A New English Dictionary on Historical Principles,* ed. Sir James A. H. Murray, Vol. 6, pt. 2, (Oxford: The Clarendon Press, 1909) 680–81. The term appeared in a 1972 publication, *Oxford Life in Oxford Archives* by W. A. Pantin (Oxford: Clarendon Press, 1972), where the author observes in his discussion of various methods used for financing professorships and lectureships: ''Most appropriators nowadays hear more about the cost of new pinnacles on a chancel or the ravages of the death-watch beetle than about the profits of tithes and mortuaries'' (46–47).

15. E. A. J. Honigmann, *Shakespeare: The ''Lost Years''* (Manchester, U.K., and Dover, N.H.: Manchester University Press) 19.

16. Robert E. Rodes, Jr., *Ecclesiastical Administration in Medieval England: The Anglo Saxons to the Reformation* (Notre Dame/London: University of Notre Dame Press, 1977) 22, and F. M. Stenton, *Anglo-Saxon England,* 3d ed. (Oxford: Clarendon Press, 1943; 1971) 152, respectively.

17. Michael Sheehan, *The Will in Medieval England: From the Conversion of the Anglo-Saxons to the End of the Thirteenth Century* (Toronto: Pontifical Institute of Mediaeval Studies, 1963) 79.

18. *OED,* Vol. 9 (London: Clarendon Press, 1933; rpt. 1970) 192, and Vol. 10, 464–65. See also *Councils and Synods,* ed. Dorothy Whitelock et al. (Oxford: Clarendon Press, 1981), 64. Selections from the laws of Canute, 1:458–506, especially p. 477, *sawlsceat:* "to minster to which it belonged." To demonstrate to the reader the irregularity of form for the term *soul-scot,* I shall include all the variant spellings as they appear in individual texts.

19. F. Liebermann, ed., *Die Gesetze der Angelsachsen,* 3 vols. (Halle a S.: May Niemeyer, 1898–1906) vol. 2, 634.

20. Joseph Bosworth, *The Anglo-Saxon Dictionary,* ed. T. Northcote Toller (Oxford: Clarendon Press, 1898) 819.

21. *Lincoln Wills* xxiii, and *Commentaries* 2:425, n. u.

22. T. F. T. Plucknett, *A Concise History of the Common Law,* 5th ed. (Boston: Little, Brown, 1956) 739.

23. Pol & Mait n. 5; Glanvill vii, 5; Bracton 338–39, n. 60. See also Sheehan 296.

24. William Easterby, *The History of the Law of Tithes in England* (Cambridge: Cambridge University Press, 1888) 19.

25. See fn. 16.

26. See *Eng Hist Doc* 1:365, and Stubbs, *SEAALH* 1:250. Anyone who did not pay by this date was liable for sixty shillings and required to render it twelvefold. For date see *Eng Hist Doc* 1:371, n. 2. According to Henry Soames, in *The Anglo-Saxon Church: Its History, Revenues, and General Character,* the monetary value of the sceat was the equivalent of ten sticas; eight was worth a modern (of Soames's time) penny (London: John W. Parker, 1844), 9, n. 16.

27. (London: Records Commission, 1840) 297, according to the personal signature numbering entered by Dr. Bosworth.

28. 2 vols. (London: Longman, Brown, Green and Longmans, 1849) Appendix B.

29. *The Homilies of Wulfstan,* ed. Dorothy Bethurum (Oxford: Clarendon Press) 229–30.

30. Ralph Houlbrooke, *Church Courts and the People During the English Reformation 1520–1570* (Oxford: Oxford University Press, 1979) 124–25. Sheehan notes a correction made by F. M. Stenton of J. Lingard's *History and Antiquities of the Anglo-Saxon Church,* where it was erroneously presented that soul-scot "was always distinguished from other charitable bequests" (Sheehan n. 27). Sheehan states categorically that the mortuary or second-best chattel "was demanded as an offering for his [the testator's] wife" (300).

31. John Godfrey, *The Church in Anglo-Saxon England* (Cambridge: Cambridge University Press, 1962) 324–25.

32. John Kemble, *The Saxons in England* (London: Longman, Brown, Green and Longmans, 1849) n. 3. See also Stubbs, on the transmission of the Penitentials under the Irish in the West and "John the Faster" in the East in the mid-sixth century (the same century in which Justinian completed the body of civil law) and on their being analogous to the early laws of Anglo-Saxon kings (*SEAALH* 1:252–53).

33. *The Geneva Bible, A facsimile of the 1560 edition* (Madison, Milwaukee, London: The University of Wisconsin Press, 1969). Shakespeare's use and knowledge of the Bible, in particular the Genevan version, is demonstrated in Richard Noble's *Shakespeare's Biblical Knowledge* (London & New York: The Macmillan Co., 1935) esp. 64ff; Alexander, 228ff; and Fripp, 69–71.

34. Compare the various forms of *best* and *second best* in the Old Testament (see James Strong, *A Concise Dictionary of the Words in the Hebrew Bible,* in Strong's *Exhaustive Concordance of the Bible* (New York and Nashville: Abingdon Press, 1890) 35, 65, 45, 119. *Best:* zimrâh זִמְרָה pruned (i.e. choice) fruit, best fruit; from *zâmar,* to prune, to trim; identical to *zimrâh,* a musical piece or song to be accompanied by an instrument, melody, psalm; from *zâmar,* to touch the strings or parts of an instrument, to play upon it, to celebrate in song and give praise. *Mêytâb* מֵיטָב the best part; from *yâṭab,* to make well, glad, be (make) better, benefit, be (make) merry. *Tôwb* טוֹב a good thing, goods; from *ṭôwb,* to be (do or make) good. *Second-best: shênîy* שֵׁנִי double, i.e., second, again; from *shânâh* = to fold, i.e., duplicate (lit. or fig.), by implication to transmute, repeat, return, alter, be given to change.

On Jewish ties to Anglo-Saxons and thence to England, see Edward Hine, *The Anglo-Saxon Riddle; or, The Riddle of Our Origin, Present Greatness, and Future Grandeur* (London: 1872), where he traces the Anglo-Saxons to the Israelites, the ten tribes as opposed to Judah, and he alludes to the work of Mr. Sharon Turner who traced the origins of the Anglo-Saxons to Media and Assyria, the place to which the ten tribes were taken captive. On Christianity as heir to Judaism, see also W. H. C. Frend, "The Rise of Christianity," *American Scholar* (1985) 397–402. For bibliographical references and a very fine series of essays first presented as papers at the Center for Medieval and Early Renaissance Studies, State University of New York at Binghamton, see Paul E. Szarmach, ed., *Aspects of Jewish Culture in the Middle Ages* (Albany, NY: SUNY Press, 1979), esp. the bibliographical references in Yosef Hayim Yerushalmi, "Medieval Jewry: From Within and From Without," 1 and 11.

35. *The principall lawes and statutes of Englande* (London: Rycharde Bankes, 1542), fols. lxx–lxxi. The 1625 edition corrected and amended appeared under the title *Institutions,* or *Principall grounds of Lawes and statutes of England* (London: Companie of Stationers, 1625). See also *Commentaries* 427, and *Calender of Wills* 1:vii. *Tithes & Oblations* (1595) also refers to the problems: "The payment of Disines [also Decimes in other places] or Tithes to the Priestes, is of the law of God . . . but . . . by reason of which converting and

altering of Tithes, there hath been in times paste, and there doeth daylie . . . growe manie controversies doubtes and questions'' (2–3). See also William Lambarde, *Eirenarcha; or, Of the Office of the Justices of Peace and The duties of Constables, Tythingmen & Church-wardens* (London: Stationers, 1614), 435, for the same restriction against such abuses and the forfeit: ''so much as he shall take over: & loose xl.*s*. to the partie grieved.''

36. Margaret Deanesly, *The Pre-Conquest Church in England: An Ecclesiastical History of England,* Vol. 1 (New York: Oxford University Press, 1943) 212, 310.

37. For note on ''law-book,'' see 431. Whitelock cites Archbishop Wulfstan's reference to the so-called laws of Edward and Guthrum in which for the first time the church due of *leohtgesceot* is introduced, ''lacking from all documents before 1008'' (pt. 9, 17). On the derivations of codes from Edgar's code (those of Canute from Aethelred, etc.) and penalties for nonpayment of *cyricsceat,* see ''Wulfstan and the Laws of Cnut'' (pt. 12, 445).

CHAPTER FIVE

1. Charles William Wallace, ''New Shakespeare Discoveries: Shakespeare as a Man Among Men,'' *Harper's Monthly Magazine* 120 (March 1910):505–06.

2. James O. Halliwell, Charles Knight, and John Payne Collier, eds., *The Complete Works of Shakespeare* (New York: Johnson, Fry, n.d.) xlv.

3. (New York: New York University Press, 1961) 23-24.

4. Bentley, *Shakespeare: A Biographical Handbook* (New Haven: Yale University Press, 1961) 43.

5. Joseph Quincy Adams, *A Life of William Shakespeare* (Boston: Houghton Mifflin, 1923) 482.

6. C. Charlotte Stopes, *Shakespeare's Warwickshire Contemporaries* (Stratford-on-Avon: Shakespeare Head Press, 1907; rpt. AMS, 1973) 176.

7. ''The first authentic report of Shakespeare as an actor appears in the accounts of the Treasurer of the Chamber for March 1594–5 . . before Queen Elizabeth at Greenwich Palace. . . . At an earlier date, when the company was under the patronage of Lord Leicester, Shakespeare was probably a member travelling with it to many towns in the Kingdom'' (Gray 121). But Gray gives 1582 as ''the more trustworthy of the traditions . . . that Shakespeare left for London at 'about eighteen' . . . soon or after the date of the licence'' (116). He thinks the couple were undoubtedly incompatible. Rowe ''gives 1585 as the earliest and 1588 as the latest date for the commencement of an absence from Stratford'' (in Gray 92). Halliwell-Phillipps assigned the year 1585—because of poaching and Sir Thomas Lucy's charge and prosecution (*Life Abb* 38). Schoenbaum thinks it ''uncertain'' but probable that by 1592 he ''had begun making his mark as a dramatist'' (*Comp Doc Life* 159 ff.). Certainly by 1594 he was a professional. But the interval between 1585 and 1592 ''scholarship

has designated the Lost Years'' (*Comp Doc Life* 95). Still another hypothesis gives 1586–87 as Shakespeare's time of departure due to anti-Papist persecution and charges against some relatives of his mother in 1583 (when there was a ''strenuous search for recusants in and around Stratford''), and also the poaching incident involving Sir Thomas Lucy of Charlecote, a very zealous anti-Papist (Speaight 23–24).

8. 1594–96 *King John;* 1595–96 *Romeo and Juliet;* 1596–97 *1 Henry IV;* 1597 *Merry Wives of Windsor;* 1598 *2 Henry IV;* 1598–99 *Much Ado about Nothing;* 1599 *Henry V, Julius Caesar, As You Like It;* 1600–1601 *Hamlet;* 1601 *The Phoenix and the Turtle;* 1601–2 *Twelfth Night, Troilus and Cressida;* 1602–3 *All's Well That Ends Well;* 1604 *Measure for Measure, Othello;* 1605 *King Lear;* 1606 *Macbeth;* 1606–7 *Antony and Cleopatra;* 1607–8 *Coriolanus;* and between 1608 and his death in 1616 appeared *Timon of Athens* (left unfinished), *Pericles, Cymbeline, The Winter's Tale, The Tempest, Henry VIII, Cardenio* (lost), and *Two Noble Kinsmen*. Chambers's dates differ: *Coriol-Timon* 1607–8; *Pericles* 1608–9; *Cymbeline* 1609–10; *Winter's Tale* 1610–11; *Tempest* 1611–12; *Henry VIII* 1612–13.

9. G. K. Chesterton, *Chesterton on Shakespeare,* ed. Dorothy Collins (Henley-on-Thames: Darwen Finlayson, 1971) 189.

Works Cited

Abbott, L. W. *Law Reporting in England 1485–1585*. London: The Athlone Press, 1972.

Adams, Joseph Quincy. *A Life of William Shakespeare*. Boston, New York: Houghton Mifflin, 1923.

———. "A New Signature of Shakespeare?" *Bulletin of the John Rylands Library, Manchester* 27(1943):256–59.

Alexander, Peter. *Shakespeare's Life and Art*. NY: New York University Press, 1961.

Andrews, Mark Edwin. *Law versus Equity in "The Merchant of Venice."* Boulder: University of Colorado Press, 1965.

Anglo-Saxon Wills. Edited with translation and notes by Dorothy Whitelock. Cambridge: Cambridge University Press, 1930.

Aubrey, John. *Brief Lives*. Ed. Oliver Lawson Dick. London: Secker and Warburg, 1949; rpt. Middlesex, England: Penguin Books, 1982.

Bartlett, John. *A Complete Concordance of Shakespeare*. New York: Macmillan, St. Martin's Press, 1966.

Bentley, Gerald Eades. *Shakespeare: A Biographical Handbook*. New Haven: Yale University Press, 1961.

Berk's Oxon & c. Chipping Norton Register. MS. Bodleian Caps 6.24.

Black, Henry Campbell. *Black's Law Dictionary*. 5th ed. St. Paul, Minn.: West Publishing Co., 1979.

Blackstone, Sir William. *Commentaries on the Laws of England: A Facsimile of the First Edition of 1765–1769*. Vol. II: *Of the Rights of Things* (1766). Introd. by A. W. Brian Simpson. Chicago and London: University of Chicago Press, 1979.

Bouvier, John. *Bouvier's Law Dictionary*. 3rd ed. Kansas City, Mo.: Vernon Law Book Co., and St. Paul, Minn.: West Publishing Co., 1914.

Bosworth, Joseph. *The Anglo-Saxon Dictionary*. Ed. T. Northcote Toller. Oxford: Clarendon Press, 1898.

Boyd, William K. "The Ecclesiastical Edicts of the Theodosian Code." *Studies in History, Economics, and Public Law*, Vol. 24, no. 63. New York: Columbia University Press, 1905.

Bracton on the Laws and Customs of England. (Original *De Legibus et Consuetudinibus Angliae*, 1640.) Translated with revisions and notes by Samuel E. Thorne. Vol. II. Cambridge: Belknap Press of Harvard University Press, published in association with the Selden Society, 1968.

Brainerd, Barron. "Pronouns and Genre in Shakespeare's Drama." *Computers and the Humanities* 13 (1979):3–16.

Bretnor, Thomas. *A Newe Almanacke and Prognostication for the yeare of our Lord God, 1616*. London: Stationer's, 1616.

Brinkworth, E.R.C. *Shakespeare and the Bawdy Court of Stratford*. London and Chichester: Phillimore, 1972.

Brooks, C. W. *Pettyfoggers and Vipers of the Commonwealth: The 'Lower Branch' of the Legal Profession in Early Modern England*. Cambridge: Cambridge University Press, 1986.

Burgess, J. Tom. *Historic Warwickshire*. Ed. Joseph Hill. 2nd ed. Birmingham, Leicester, Leamington, and London, 1893.

The Calendar of Wills, Proved and Enrolled in the Court of Husting, London, A.D. 1258–A.D. 1688. Ed. Reginald R. Sharpe. Part II: *A.D. 1358–A.D. 1688*. London: John C. Francis, 1890.

The Cambridge Companion to Shakespeare Studies. Ed. Stanley Wells. Cambridge: Cambridge University Press, 1986.

Cameron, J. M. "Between the Character and the Role." *TLS*, July 3, 1981, 743–44. (Review of John Bayley, *Shakespeare and Tragedy*.)

Campbell, Lord John. *Shakespeare's Legal Acquirements Considered*. New York: D. Appleton and Co., 1859.

Chambers, E. K. *William Shakespeare: A Study of Facts and Problems*. Vols. 1 and 2. Oxford: Clarendon Press, 1930.

Chesterton, G. K. *Chesterton on Shakespeare*. Ed. Dorothy Collins. Henley-on-Thames: Darwen Finlayson, 1971.

Chute, Marchette. "Shakespeare—Husband, Actor." *Wisdom* 1, no. 1 (January 1956):20–23.

Clarke, Charles, and Mary Cowden. *The Shakespeare Key*. New York: Frederick Ungar, 1961.

Coke, Sir Edward. *The First Part of the Institutes of the Lawes of England; or, A Commentarie upon Littleton, not the name of a Lawyer onely, but of the Law it selfe*. 2d ed. London: John More, 1629.

———. *The Third and Fourth Part of the Institutes of the Laws of England.*

New York & London: Garland, 1979. Rpt. of 1628 ed. printed by M. Flesher and W. Lee for D. Pakeman, London.

Corpus Juris Civilis. "De Testamentis Ordinandis." Tit. X. Scholia in Instit. Lib. II. Ed. Paulas Krueger. Berlin, 1905.

Cosin, Richard. *An Apologie of and for Sundrie Proceedings by Jurisdiction Ecclesiasticall, of late times by some challenged, and also diversly by them impugned*. London, 1591.

Councils and Synods: With Other Documents Relating to the English Church. Ed. D. Whitelock, M. Brett, and C.N.L. Brooke. Vol. 1, pt. 1:*871–1066;* pt. 2:*1066–1204*. Oxford: Clarendon Press, 1981.

Cowell, John. *The Interpreter; or, Booke Containing the Signification of Words*. Cambridge, 1607; 1708, rpt. Amsterdam, New York: Da Capo Press, 1970.

Dadc, William. *A new Almanacke and Prognostication, with the Foiraine Computation, in which you may behold the state of this yeare of our Lord God 1616. Being Leape yeare*. London: Stationers, 1616.

Dawson, Giles E. "Authenticity and Attribution of Written Matter." *English Institute Annual, 1942*. New York: Columbia University Press, 1943.

Deanesly, Margaret. *The Pre-Conquest Church in England: An Ecclesiastical History of England*. Vol. I. New York: Oxford University Press, 1961.

The Dictionary of National Biography. Eds. Sir Leslie Stephen and Sir Sidney Lee. Oxford: Oxford University Press, 1917.

Drew, C. *Early Parochial Organization in England: The Origins of the Office of Churchwarden*. York: St. Anthony's Hall Publication no. 7, 1954.

Dugdale, Sir William. *Monasticon Anglicanum: A History of the Abbies and Other Monasteries, Hospitals, Frieries, and Cathedral and 38 Collegiate Churches with their Dependencies in England and Wales*. Trans. and ed. John Caley, Henry Ellis, Rev. Bulkeley Bandinel. Vol. 1. London: Longman, 1817–19.

Dunkel, Wilbur. *William Lambarde, Elizabethan Jurist, 1536–1601*. New Brunswick: Rutgers University Press, 1965.

Early English Manuscripts in Facsimile, Vol. 17: *A Wulfstan Manuscript* (British Museum Cotton Nero A. 1). Ed. Henry R. Loyn. Copenhagen: Rosenkilde and Bagger, 1971.

Easterby, William. *The History of the Law of Tithes in England*. Cambridge: Cambridge University Press, 1888.

Eccles, Mark. *Shakespeare in Warwickshire*. Madison: University of Wisconsin Press, 1961.

Elton, Geoffrey Rudolph. *England, 1200–1640: The Sources of History*. Ithaca: Cornell University Press, 1969.

Elton, W. R. "Shakespeare and the thought of his age," in *The Cambridge Companion to Shakespeare Studies*. Ed. Stanley Wells. Cambridge: Cambridge University Press, 1986, 17–35.

Emmison, Frederick George. *Elizabethan Life: Home, Work, and Land.* Chelmsford: Essex County Council, and Plymouth, Mass.: Pilgrim Society and Plimoth Plantation, 1976.

———. *Elizabethan Life: Morals and the Church Courts.* Chelmsford: Essex County Council, 1973.

Encyclopedia Britannica. Vol. 4. 1988 ed. 145.

English Historical Documents, c. 500–1042. Ed. Dorothy Whitelock. London: English History, 1955.

Everitt, E. B. *The Young Shakespeare: Studies in Documentary Evidence. Anglistica,* Vol. 2. Ed. Torsten Dahl, Kemp Malone, and Geoffrey Tillotson. Copenhagen: Rosenkilde and Bagger, 1954.

Foster, John. *A Shakespeare Word-Book.* New York: Russell and Russell, 1908 (reissue 1968).

Fox, Levi. "An Early Copy of Shakespeare's Will." *Shakespeare Survey* 4 (1951):69–77.

French, George Russell. *Shakspeareana Genealogica.* London and Cambridge: Macmillan, 1869.

Frend, W.H.C. "The Rise of Christianity." *American Scholar* (1985):397–402.

Fripp, Edgar I. *Shakespeare's Stratford.* London: Oxford University Press, Humphrey Milford, 1928.

Furnivall, F. J. *The Fifty Earliest English Wills in the Court of Probate, London.* London: Trubner & Co., 1882.

———. *The Royal Shakespere.* 3 vols. London, Paris, and New York: Cassell, 1880.

The Geneva Bible, A facsimile of the 1560 edition. Madison, Milwaukee, London: The University of Wisconsin Press, 1969.

Glanvill. *The treatise on the laws and customs of the realm of England commonly called Glanvill.* Ed. G.D.G. Hall. London: Thomas Nelson and Sons in association with the Selden Society, 1965.

Gless, Darryl J. *Measure for Measure, the Law, and the Convent.* Princeton, N.J.: Princeton University Press, 1979.

Godfrey, John. *The Church in Anglo-Saxon England.* Cambridge: Cambridge University Press, 1962.

Gray, Joseph William. *Shakespeare's Marriage.* London: Chapman & Hall, 1905; New York: AMS, 1973.

Greaves, Richard L. *Society and Religion in Elizabethan England.* Minneapolis: University of Minnesota Press, 1981.

Green, A. Wigfall. "Shakespeare's Will." *Georgetown Law Journal* 20(March 1932):273–92.

Greene, Reverend Joseph. *Correspondence of the Reverend Joseph Greene: Parson, Schoolmaster, and Antiquary (1712–1790).* Ed. Levi Fox. London: Stationery Office, 1965.

Hall, E. Vine. *Testamentary Papers II: Wills from Shakespeare's Town and Time*. 2d ser. London: Mitchell Hughes and Clarke, 1933.

Halliwell, James O. *Shakespeare's Will*. London: John Russell Smith, 1851.

———. *The Works of William Shakespeare*. Vol. 1: *The Life of Shakespeare*. Illus. F. W. Fairholt. London: C. and J. Adlard, 1853.

Halliwell-Phillipps, James O. *The Life of William Shakespeare: Abbreviated*. New York: Bigelow Smith, 1909.

———. *Outlines of the Life of Shakespeare*. 10th ed. Vol. 1. London, New York, Bombay: Longmans, Green, 1898.

Hamilton, Charles. *In Search of Shakespeare: A Reconnaissance into the Poet's Life and Handwriting*. San Diego, New York, London: Harcourt Brace Jovanovich, 1985.

Hanley, Hugh A. "Shakespeare's Family in Stratford Records." *The Times Literary Supplement* (May 21, 1964), 441.

Heal, Felicity, and Rosemary O'Day, eds. *Continuity and Change: Personnel and Administration of the Church in England 1500–1642*. London: Leicester University Press, 1976.

Helmholz, R. H. *Roman Canon Law in Reformation England*. Cambridge: Cambridge University Press, 1990.

Hirsch, E. D., Jr. *Validity in Interpretation*. New Haven & London: Yale University Press, 1967.

Holdsworth, Sir William. *A History of English Law*. 9 Vols. Vol. 3. London: Methuen, Sweet and Maxwell, 1908; rpt. 1966.

The Homilies of Wulfstan. Ed. Dorothy Bethurum. Oxford: Clarendon Press, 1957.

Honigmann, E.A.J. *Shakespeare: The "Lost Years."* Manchester, U.K., and Dover, New Hampshire: Manchester University Press, 1985.

Hotson, Leslie. *I, William Shakespeare*. London: Jonathan Cape, 1937.

Houlbrooke, Ralph. *Church Courts and the People During the English Reformation 1520–1570*. Oxford: Oxford University Press, 1979.

Howells, William Dean. *The Seen and Unseen at Stratford-on-Avon: A Fantasy*. New York: Harper & Bros., 1914.

Ingram, Martin. *Church Courts, Sex and Marriage in England, 1570–1640*. Cambridge: Cambridge University Press, 1987; repr. 1988.

Johansson, Bertil. *Law and Lawyers in Elizabethan England*. Stockholm: Almquist & Wiksell, 1967.

Keeton, George W. *English Law: The Judicial Contribution*. New Abbot Devon: David & Charles, 1974.

Kemble, John Mitchell. *The Saxons in England*. 2 vols. London: Longman, Brown, Green and Longmans, 1849.

Kermode, Frank, ed. *The Winter's Tale*. In *The Complete Signet Classic Shakespeare*. Sylvan Barnet, General Editor. New York, Chicago, San Francisco, Atlanta: Harcourt Brace Jovanovich, 1972.

Knight, W. Nicholas. *Shakespeare's Hidden Life: Shakespeare at the Law, 1585–1595*. New York: Mason and Lipscomb, 1973.

Lambarde, William. *APXAIONOMIA, sive De Priscis Anglorum legibus, Saxon. et Lat*. Bodleian Catalogue: Douce Collection L. 196. London: John Davis, 1568; Folger Shakespeare Library, 1568, microfilm of Shakespeare signature copy.

———. *Eirenarcha; or, Of the Office of the Justices of Peace & The duties of Constables, Tythingmen & Church-wardens*. London: Stationers, 1614.

The Laws of the Kings of England from Edmund to Henry I. Ed. A. J. Robertson. Cambridge: Cambridge University Press, 1925.

Lee, Sidney. *A Life of William Shakespeare*. 4th ed. London: John Murray, 1925.

Levi, Peter. *The Life and Times of William Shakespeare*. London: Macmillan, 1988.

Levine, Joseph M. "Tudor Antiquaries." *History Today* 20 (1970):278–85.

Lewis, Benjamin Roland. *The Shakespeare Documents*. 2 vols. Stanford: Stanford University Press, and London: Oxford University Press, 1941.

Liebermann, F., ed. *Die Gesetze der Angelsachsen*. 3 vols. Halle A.S: Max Niemeyer, 1898–1906.

Lincoln Wills. Vol. 2: *A.D. 1505–May 1530*. Ed. C. W. Foster. Horncastle: W. K. Morton and Sons, 1918.

Lyndwood, William. *Provinciale (Constitutions of Lambeth)*, Oxford: Hall and Davis, 1679.

Maitland, Frederic William. *English Law and the Renaissance* (The Rede Lecture for 1901). Cambridge: Cambridge University Press, 1901.

Malone, Edmond. *Shakespeare, Plays and Poems*, 10 vols. London: J. Rivington & Sons, 1790.

Marcham, Frank. *William Shakespeare and His Daughter Susannah*. London: Grafton & Co., 1931.

McManaway, James G. "John Shakespeare's 'Spiritual Testament.' " *Shakespeare Quarterly* 18(1967):197–205.

Middle English Dictionary. Vol. 7. Ed. Sherman Kuhn. Ann Arbor: University of Michigan Press, 1975.

Milward, Peter, S. J. *Shakespeare's Religious Background*. London: Sidgwick and Jackson, 1973.

Murray, Sir James. *New English Dictionary*. Oxford: Clarendon Press, 1933.

Mutschmann, H., and K. Wentersdorf. *Shakespeare and Catholicism*. New York: Sheed and Ward, 1952.

Mynsinger, Joachimi a Frundeck. *Institutionum Iuris Civilis*. London, 1579, 1679.

A New English Dictionary on Historical Principles, Vol. 6, pt. 2. Ed. Sir James A. H. Murray. Oxford: The Clarendon Press, 1909.

Noble, Richard. *Shakespeare's Biblical Knowledge*. London & New York: The Macmillan Co., 1935.

Nowell, Laurence. *Vocabularium Saxonicum*. Ed. Albert H. Marckwardt. Ann Arbor: University of Michigan Press, 1952.

The Oxford English Dictionary. Prepared by J. A. Simpson and E.S.C. Weiner. 2nd ed. Oxford: Clarendon Press, 1989.

Pantin, W. A. *Oxford Life in Oxford Archives*. Oxford: Clarendon Press, 1972.

Perrow, Eber Carle. "The Last Will and Testament as a Form of Literature." *Transactions of the Wisconsin Academy of Sciences, Arts, and Letters* 17, 1(1914):682–750.

Phillips, O. Hood. *Shakespeare and the Lawyers*. London: Methuen, 1972.

Plucknett, T.F.T. *A Concise History of the Common Law*. 5th ed. Boston: Little, Brown, 1956.

———. *Early English Legal Literature*. Cambridge: Cambridge University Press, 1958.

Pollock, Sir Frederick, and Frederic William Maitland. *The History of English Law before the Time of Edward I*. 2d ed. Vols. 1–3. Cambridge: Cambridge University Press, 1968.

The principall lawes and statutes of Englande, whyche be at thys present day in use, compendiously gathered together for the weale & benefyt of the kynges Maiesties most lovying subiectes, newly recognized and augmented. London: Rycharde Bankes, 1542.

Ranald, Margaret Loftus. " 'As Marriage Binds, and Blood Breaks': English Marriage and Shakespeare." *Shakespeare Quarterly* 30, no. 1 (Winter 1979):68–81.

Rastell, John. *An Exposition of Certaine Difficult and Obscure Words, and Terms of the Lawes of This Realme . . . unto are also added the Old Tenures*. London: Richard Tottell, 1572; 1579; 1592; 1598; 1609.

Reese, M. M. *Shakespeare, His World and His Work*. London: Edward Arnold Publishers Ltd., 1953; rev. ed. 1980.

The Riverside Shakespeare. Ed. G. Blakemore Evans. Boston: Houghton Mifflin, 1974.

Robertson, A. J. *Anglo-Saxon Charters*. Cambridge: Cambridge University Press, 1939.

Rodes, Robert E., Jr. *Ecclesiastical Administration in Medieval England: The Anglo-Saxons to the Reformation*. Notre Dame and London: University of Notre Dame Press, 1977.

Rowse, A. L. *William Shakespeare: A Biography*. New York and Evanston: Harper and Row, 1963.

———. "Will's Testament: The Bard as Biographer." *Wall Street Journal*, April 22, 1983.

Rudstone, John. *An Almanacke and Prognostication for the yeere of our Lord God 1616*. London: Stationers Co., 1616.

Rushton, William. *Shakespeare: A Lawyer.* Liverpool: Webb & Hunt, 1858; repr. New York: AMS Press, 1977.

Schoeck, R. J. "Canon Law in England on the Eve of the Reformation," *Mediaeval Studies,* 25(1963):125–147.

———. "Early Anglo-Saxon Studies and Legal Scholarship in the Renaissance." *Studies in the Renaissance* 5(1958):102–10.

———. "Recent Scholarship in the History of Law." *Renaissance Quarterly* 20(1967):279–91.

Schoenbaum, S. *Shakespeare: The Globe and the World.* New York, Oxford, Toronto, Melbourne: Folger Shakespeare Library, Oxford University Press, 1979.

———. *Shakespeare's Lives.* Oxford. Clarendon Press, and New York: Oxford University Press, 1970.

———. *William Shakespeare: A Compact Documentary Life.* New York: Oxford University Press, 1977.

———. *William Shakespeare: A Documentary Life.* Oxford: Clarendon Press in association with the Scolar Press, 1975.

———. *William Shakespeare: Records and Images.* New York: Oxford University Press, 1981.

Select Essays in Anglo-American Legal History. 3 vols. Boston: Little, Brown, 1909.

Alice Stopford Green, "The Centralization of Norman Justice under Henry II," 1:111–39.

Edward Jenks, "Edward I, The English Justinian," 1:139–68.

Frederic William Maitland, "English Law and the Renaissance," 1:168–208.

William Stubbs, "The History of the Canon Law in England," 1:248–89.

Heinrich Brunner, "The Sources of English Law," 2:7–53.

William Searle Holdsworth, "The Ecclesiastical Courts and Their Jurisdiction," 2:255–312.

Melville Madison Bigelow, "The Rise of the English Will," 3:770–82.

Seng, Peter J. *The Vocal Songs in the Plays of Shakespeare: A Critical History.* Cambridge: Harvard University Press, 1967.

Shakespeare in the Public Records. Ed. David Thomas and Jane Cox. London: Her Majesty's Stationery Office, 1985.

Shakespeare, William. *The Complete Works of Shakespeare.* Ed. James O. Halliwell, Charles Knight, and John Payne Collier. Vol. 3. New York: Johnson, Fry, n.d.

———. *The Complete Works of Shakespeare.* Ed. G. Blakemore Evans. Boston: Houghton Mifflin, 1974.

———. *The First Folio of Shakespeare* (Facsimile). Prepared by Charlton Hinman. New York: W. W. Norton & Co., Inc., 1968.

Sheehan, Michael M., C.S.B. *The Will in Medieval England: From the Con-*

version of the Anglo-Saxons to the End of the Thirteenth Century. Toronto: Pontifical Institute of Mediaeval Studies, 1963.

Simpson, Frank. "New Place: The Only Representation of Shakespeare's House, from an Unpublished MS." *Shakespeare Survey* 5 (1952):55–57.

Sisam, Kenneth. *Studies in the History of Old English Literature*. Oxford: Clarendon Press, 1953.

Smith, J. A. Clarence. *Medieval Law Teachers and Writers, Civilian and Canonist*. Ottawa, Canada: University of Ottawa Press, 1975.

Soames, Henry. *The Anglo-Saxon Church: Its History, Revenues, and General Character*. London: John W. Parker, 1844.

Southern, A. C. *Elizabethan Recusant Prose: 1559–1582*. London: Sands, 1950.

Speaight, Robert. *Shakespere: The Man and His Achievement*. London: J. M. Dent and Sons, 1977.

Spevack, Marvin. *A Complete and Systematic Concordance to the Works of Shakespeare*. Vol. 6: *A Concordance to the Complete Works*. Hildesheim: Georg Olms, 1970.

Stenton, Doris M. *The English Woman in History*. London: Allen and Unwin; New York: Macmillan, 1957.

Stenton, Frank M. *Anglo-Saxon England*. 3d. ed. Oxford: Clarendon Press, 1943; 1971.

Stopes, Charlotte Carmichael. *Shakespeare's Warwickshire Contemporaries*. Stratford-upon-Avon: Shakespeare Head Press, 1907; rpt. New York: AMS Press, 1973.

Stubbs, William. *The Constitutional History of England*. Vol. 1. Oxford: Clarendon Press, 1897.

Swinburne, Henry. *A Briefe Treatise of Testaments and Last Willes*. London: John Windet, 1568 (4° R of Th. Douce SS 111, Bodleian Library Catalogue); 2d ed. 1590 (4° A. 30 Jur. Bodleian Library Catalogue). London: Stationers', 1611, 1635.

———. *A Treatise of Spousals, or Matrimonial Contracts; Wherein All the Questions relating to that Subject are ingeniously Debated and Resolved*. London: Printed by S. Roycroft for Robert Clavell at the Peacock in St. Paul's Church-yard, 1606 (4° R. 87 Th.), 1686.

Thorpe, Benjamin. *The Ancient Laws and Institutes of England*. Vol. 2. London: Records Commission, 1840.

Tithes & Oblations, according to the Laws Established by the Church of England. 8° [n.p.] 1595.

Upcote, Augustine. *An Almanacke and Prognostication for this yeare of our Lord God 1616. Being the Bissextile or leape yeare*. London: Stationers Co., 1616.

Wagenknecht, Edward. *The Personality of Shakespeare*. Norman Okla.: University of Oklahoma Press, 1972.

Wallace, Charles William. "New Shakespeare Discoveries: Shakespeare as a Man Among Men." *Harper's Monthly Magazine* 120 (March 1910):489–510.

Whitelock, Dorothy. *Anglo-Saxon Wills.* Cambridge: Cambridge University Press, 1930.

———. *History, Law, and Literature in 10th–11th Century England.* London: Variorum Reprints, 1981.

Williams, Charles. *A Short Life of Shakespeare; An Abridgement of E. K. Chambers, William Shakespeare: A Study of Facts and Problems.* Oxford: Oxford University Press, n.d.

Winfield, Percy H. *The Chief Sources of English Legal History.* Cambridge, Mass.: Harvard University Press, 1925.

Woodcock, Brian L. *Medieval Ecclesiastical Courts in the Diocese of Canterbury.* London: Oxford University Press, Geoffrey Cumberlege, 1952.

Woodhouse, John. *A plaine Almanacke or Prognostication for the yeere of our Lord God 1616.* London: Stationers Co., 1616.

Wunderli, Richard M. *London Church Courts and Society on the Eve of the Reformation.* Cambridge, Mass.: Medieval Academy of America, 1981.

Index

About the Author

JOYCE ROGERS is Associate Professor, Religious Studies Program, University of New Mexico, and the author of *Louis Martin: Father of a Saint* and co-author of *Thought to Essay*.